THE LAW COMMISSION

DOMESTIC VIOLENCE A
OCCUPATION OF THE FAMIL

TABLE OF CONTENTS

THE LAW COMMISSION

Item 6 of the Fourth Programme: Family Law

DOMESTIC VIOLENCE AND OCCUPATION OF THE FAMILY HOME

*To the Right Honourable the Lord Mackay of Clashfern,
Lord High Chancellor of Great Britain*

PART I

INTRODUCTION

The range and aims of this project

1.1 This report makes recommendations for reform of the various discretionary remedies which exist in family law to deal with two distinct but inseparable problems: providing protection for one member of a family against molestation or violence by another and regulating the occupation of the family home where the relationship has broken down whether temporarily or permanently. A draft Bill to implement these recommendations appears in Appendix A. This report forms part of the "comprehensive examination of family law . . . with a view to its systematic reform and eventual codification" prescribed by Item 6 of our Fourth Programme of Law Reform.[1] It follows the publication for consultation in 1989 of a working paper[2] which examined in some detail the current law and practice and the criticisms which might be made of them and suggested both a number of individual reforms and a possible new structure. We are very grateful to the many people and organisations who responded to the working paper for their ideas and contributions and for the help they have given. A list of the respondents appears in Appendix B.

1.2 The existing civil remedies in this area have been the source of much complaint.[3] They are complex, confusing and lack integration. Lord Scarman has described the statutory provisions as "a hotchpot of enactments of limited scope passed into law to meet specific situations or to strengthen the powers of specified courts. The sooner the range, scope and effect of these powers are rationalised into a coherent and comprehensive body of statute law, the better."[4] Our aims in undertaking this project have therefore been threefold. The first is to remove the gaps, anomalies and inconsistencies in the existing remedies, with a view to synthesising them, so far as possible, into a clear, simple and comprehensive code. Secondly, we have taken it for granted that any reform should not reduce the level of protection which is available at present and might wish to improve it. Thirdly, however, it is desirable, and consistent with our work on children and divorce,[5] to seek to avoid exacerbating hostilities between the adults involved, so far as this is compatible with providing proper and effective protection both for adults and for children.

1.3 The major proposal in the working paper was that there should be a single consistent set of remedies which would be available in all courts having jurisdiction in family matters, although perhaps with some specific limitations on the magistrates' courts' powers.[6] All the respondents who commented specifically upon this issue were in favour of such a code and no-one argued against it. Accordingly, a recommendation for a comprehensive code forms the basis of this report.

---

[1] Fourth Programme of Law Reform (1989), Law Com. No. 185.

[2] Domestic Violence and Occupation of the Family Home, (1989), Working Paper No. 113.

[3] e.g. Women's National Commission, *Violence against women: report of an ad hoc working group*, (1985); S. Maidment, "Laws for Battered Women—are they an improvement?" (1977) 7 Fam. Law 50; S. D. Migdal, "Domestic Violence—Has the Act beaten it?" (1979) 9 Fam. Law 136; M. Wright, "The DVMPA 1976: An Evaluation" [1980] N.L.J. 127; A. Bainham, "Conduct and Exclusion Orders" (1980) 10 Fam. Law 228; R. Hamilton, "Has the House of Lords abolished the Domestic Violence Act for Married Women?" Legal Action, March 1984, p. 25; P. Parkinson, "The Domestic Violence Act and *Richards* v. *Richards*" (1986) 16 Fam. Law 70; S. Edwards and A. Halpern, "Conflicting Interests: Protecting Children or Protecting Title to Property" [1988] J.S.W.L. 110; J. Barron, *Not Worth the Paper . . ?* (1990).

[4] *Richards* v. *Richards* [1984] A.C. 174 at 206, 7.

[5] Family Law: Review of Child Law: Guardianship and Custody, (1988), Law Com. No. 172; Family Law: The Ground for Divorce, (1990), Law Com. No. 192.

[6] See para. 5.4 below.

The scope of the legislation

1.4 The family law remedies for domestic violence and occupation of the family home are at present provided by three different statutes[7] and by the power of the High Court and county courts to grant injunctions ancillary to some other remedy within their jurisdiction or in support of a right recognised by the general law.[8] We have not included in our review aspects of the criminal law which relate to domestic violence or of public housing law which relate to the occupation of the family home on the breakdown of the relationship. The housing law problems which have arisen are currently under consideration by a Department of the Environment Working Party[9] and it would be inappropriate for us to make recommendations about them.[10]

1.5 The draft Bill in Appendix A to this report is intended to provide a unified body of law dealing with civil remedies for molestation, violence and occupation of the family home between family members. Accordingly, it repeals the Domestic Violence and Matrimonial Proceedings Act 1976 and sections 16 to 18 of the Domestic Proceedings and Magistrates' Courts Act 1978. It also repeals the Matrimonial Homes Act 1983, although substantial parts of this have been re-enacted. These include sections 1 and 2 dealing with spouses' rights of occupation and the effects of those rights as a charge on the dwelling-house, parts of which are now to be found in clauses 4 and 5 of the draft Bill. The order-making provisions have been separated and are in clauses 7, 9 and 10. Sections 3 to 6 and 8 of the 1983 Act, dealing with registration of the charge, have been substantially re-enacted in clause 20 of and Schedule 1 to the draft Bill, and the provisions in Schedule 1 to the 1983 Act relating to the transfer of tenancies have been extended to cohabitants and re-enacted with consequential amendments, in section 19 of and Schedule 4 to the draft Bill.

1.6 Injunctions under the inherent jurisdiction are most frequently obtained ancillary to divorce or judicial separation proceedings, or, for cohabitants, ancillary to an action for assault, battery, nuisance or trespass. Whilst the continued use of these powers side by side with a new code which by definition should be comprehensive might seem undesirable, it could not be right to place restrictions on the ordinary powers available to the higher courts. However, we anticipate that the improved remedies and procedures proposed in this report and their availability in any family proceedings should eliminate the need for orders to be made under the inherent jurisdiction unless there is a particular reason for this being more appropriate.

The structure of this report

1.7 In Part II we set the social context in which civil remedies against domestic violence have become necessary, explain how the present law has developed and discuss the basic approach of the new scheme which we recommend. Our new schemes for non-molestation and occupation orders are set out in Parts III and IV respectively. Part V deals mainly with procedural matters common to both. A number of property related issues and the question of ouster orders for the protection of children in public law are covered in Part VI. Part VII collects our recommendations.

Terminology

1.8 In this report we propose, for ease of exposition, to use the genders which reflect the majority of proceedings in this jurisdiction, that is, that the applicant is a woman and the respondent a man or that the alleged attacker or molester is a man and the alleged victim a woman. Nonetheless, the reverse is sometimes the case and the remedies discussed in this report are and should be equally available to both men and women whenever the need for them arises.

---

[7] The Matrimonial Homes Act 1983, the Domestic Violence and Matrimonial Proceedings Act 1976 and the Domestic Proceedings and Magistrates' Courts Act 1978. For a more detailed account of the present law see working paper No. 113, *op. cit.*, Parts II and III and paras. 2.21–2.30 below.

[8] Supreme Court Act 1981, s.37; County Courts Act 1984, s.38.

[9] The Relationship Breakdown Working Party in which representatives of the Law Commission are participating.

[10] Although our recommendations take account of some of the problems which are briefly outlined in paras. 2.15–2.20 below.

PART II

THE CONTEXT

The social context

2.1 A large literature has developed over the past 20 years upon the problems of domestic violence, its nature, causes and extent and the effectiveness of various responses to it.[1] Domestic violence is generally thought of as taking place between husband and wife or cohabiting partners but, although this is the most common situation, violence can and not infrequently does extend also to children or others living in the same household. Whilst the phenomenon is by no means new,[2] its recognition as a major social problem dates only from the early 1970s.[3] There can be no doubt of the extent of the problem. It has been summarised thus: "all studies that exist indicate that wife abuse is a common and pervasive problem and that men from practically all countries, cultures, classes and income groups indulge in the behaviour. The issue has serious implications from both a short-term and long-term perspective and from an individual and societal perspective. Many victims suffer serious physical and psychological injury, sometimes even death, while the economic and social costs to the community are enormous and the implications for future generations impossible to estimate."[4]

(a) Nature

2.2 Although both men and women can suffer domestic violence,[5] nearly all the studies have shown that in the great majority of cases, men are the perpetrators and women are the victims.[6] In the case of homicide, the most extreme form of domestic violence, for the years between 1982 and 1987, 38%–49% of female victims, but only 5%–7% of male victims, were killed by their partners.[7] Although statistics show a concentration of violence occurring within working class families[8] many writers have challenged the notion that domestic violence is a "blue collar" phenomenon. They suggest that the stereotype of the battered wife, as young, working class and on welfare benefits, is a distortion of the true picture arising from reliance on available, visible research material, most studies having been carried out on victims in refuges. More wealthy women have more options available to them. They are less likely to use refuges or appear in social work or welfare records. There is evidence that domestic violence occurs at all levels of society and amongst people of all classes and

---

[1] For a review of this see e.g. L. J. F. Smith, *Domestic Violence: an overview of the literature*, Home Office Research Study No. 107, (1989); M. D. A. Freeman, *Violence in the Home*, (1979); Women's National Commission, *Violence against Women*, (1985); J. Clifton, "Factors Predisposing Family Members to Violence", in Social Work Services Group, Scottish Education Department, *Violence in the Family—Theory and Practice in Social Work*, (1982).

[2] T. Davidson, "Wifebeating: a recurring phenomenon throughout history", in M. Roy (ed.) *Battered Women*, (1977); M. May, "Violence in the Family: an Historical Perspective", in J. P. Martin (ed.), *Violence and the Family*, (1978), pp. 135–150.

[3] Popular awareness in this country was prompted to a large extent by E. Pizzey, *Scream Quietly or the Neighbours Will Hear*, (1974) and by media coverage of the work of Chiswick Women's Aid.

[4] United Nations Centre for Social Development and Humanitarian Affairs, *Violence against Women in the Family*, (1989), p. 97.

[5] Whilst a certain amount of attention has been paid to "battered husbands" e.g. F. Bates, "A plea for the battered husband" (1981) 11 Fam. Law 90, other commentators have concluded that whilst some husbands certainly suffer violence at the hands of their wives, this is an individual rather than a social problem. It is uncommon and there is no sound evidence to support the contention that any "syndrome" exists comparable to the problem of battered wives. See M. D. Pagelow, "The 'battered husband syndrome': social problem or much ado about little?", in N. Johnson (ed.), *Marital Violence*, (1985).

[6] Smith, *op. cit.*, pp. 2, 6–14. See also Victoria Law Reform Committee, *Homicide*, Report No. 40, (1991), appendix 2. In the latter, an analysis of Family Incident Reports completed by the Victoria Police between December 1987 and May 1988, 85% of incidents were regarded by the police as having been initiated by males, 75% against females.

[7] *Hansard* (H.C.), 12 May 1989, Vol. 152 cols. 565–566. Further, an Australian study into the reasons for spouse killings found a history of physical abuse in almost half the cases. 70% of husband killings occurred in the context of violence by the husband on the wife, 52% of which were in response to an immediate threat or attack by the husband. "Violence or fear of future violence was both the background and the cause of the use of force by women on their husbands. They killed their husbands after they or another family member had been attacked. Wife killings, on the other hand, only occurred in the context of repeated violence by the husband. It was never in itself the "reason" a man killed his wife". The Australian Law Reform Commission, *Domestic Violence*, Report No. 30, (1986), p. 1.

[8] Smith, *op. cit.*, p. 15.

backgrounds.[9] There is almost universal agreement amongst researchers that violence escalates in frequency and intensity over time,[10] and that many women suffer violence for many years before seeking outside help or going to a refuge.[11]

2.3 Domestic violence can take many forms. The term "violence" itself is often used in two senses. In its narrower meaning it describes the use of threat of physical force against a victim in the form of an assault or battery.[12] But in the context of the family, there is also a wider meaning which extends to abuse beyond the more typical instances of physical assaults to include any form of physical, sexual or psychological molestation or harassment which has a serious detrimental effect upon the health and well-being of the victim, albeit that there is no "violence" involved in the sense of physical force. Examples of such "non-violent" harassment or molestation cover a very wide range of behaviour.[13] Common instances include persistent pestering and intimidation through shouting, denigration, threats or argument, nuisance telephone calls, damaging property, following the applicant about and repeatedly calling at her home or place of work. Installing a mistress into the matrimonial home with a wife and three children,[14] filling car locks with superglue, writing anonymous letters and pressing one's face against a window whilst brandishing papers[15] have all been held to amount to molestation. The degree of severity of such behaviour depends less upon its intrinsic nature than upon it being part of a pattern and upon its effect on the victim. Acts of molestation often follow upon previous behaviour which has been violent or otherwise offensive. Calling at the applicant's house on one occasion may not be objectionable. Calling frequently and unexpectedly at unsocial hours when the victim is known to be afraid certainly is. Such forms of abuse may in some circumstances be just as harmful, vicious and distressing as physical injuries. Other forms of "non-violent" abuse, such as the sexual abuse of a child, may in the long term be more harmful.[16]

(b) Extent

2.4 The true extent of domestic violence is impossible to assess. It is possible only to build up a fragmented picture from a number of different sources of information, each of which has its own limitations. However, it is clear from the information which is available that it is a widespread problem which takes up a significant amount of court time. There is also good reason to think that a considerable amount of such violence is never brought to the courts' attention at all. As there is no settled definition of the term "domestic violence", people's interpretations of it differ. It is thought that incidents of domestic violence are infrequently reported to the police. There is a tendency for victims to try to conceal attacks for as long as possible through either a misguided sense of shame, fear of reprisals or distrust of the authorities.[17] Estimates of the proportion of incidents reported to the police are unreliable and vary widely. Figures as different as 2%, 10%, 28% and 71% have been given.[18] Moreover, official criminal statistics have been challenged as unreliable and inaccurate in their reflection of the number of cases actually reported. There is evidence that many of the cases which are reported to the police have, at least in the past,[19] gone unrecorded. Incidents which are recorded may later be omitted from the criminal statistics owing to the unwillingness of the complainant to prosecute.[20]

---

[9] United Nations, *op. cit.*, pp. 15–16; Report of U.S. Attorney General's Task Force on Violence in the Family, (1984).

[10] Smith, *op. cit.*, pp. 16–17.

[11] e.g. It has been found in Canada that women who bring criminal charges against their partners have been assaulted an average of 35 times. A. McGillivray, "Battered women: Definition, Models and Prosecution Policy", (1987) 6 Can. J. Fam. Law 15, 18.

[12] For harrowing descriptions of the abuse suffered by some women, see Report of the Select Committee on Violence in Marriage, Vol. 2, (1977), pp. 20–23, 137–141; J. Pahl, *A Refuge for Battered Women*, (1978), pp. 29–30; Cleveland Refuge and Aid for Women and Children, *Private Violence: Public Shame*, (1984), p. 4.

[13] *Vaughan* v. *Vaughan* [1973] 1 W.L.R. 1159.

[14] *Adams* v. *Adams* (1965) 109 S.J. 899.

[15] *Smith* v. *Smith* [1988] 1 F.L.R. 179.

[16] Report of the Enquiry into Child Abuse in Cleveland 1987 (Butler-Sloss Report), (1988), Cm. 412.

[17] See generally R. E. Dobash, R. P. Dobash and K. Cavanagh, "The contact between battered women and social and medical agencies" in J. Pahl (ed.), *Private Violence and Public Policy: the needs of battered women and the response of the public services*, (1985), p. 142.

[18] Smith, *op. cit.*, p. 7.

[19] A number of police forces have recently revised their policies on the reporting and treatment of domestic violence offences. For example, the Metropolitan Police set up a Working Group into Domestic Violence in 1984, which published a report in 1987 making recommendations on policy changes, enhanced support for victims, better training and better record keeping. Since 1987, 47 specialist domestic violence units have been set up within the Metropolitan district. See also Home Office Circular 60/1990.

[20] S. S. M. Edwards, "The Real Risks of Violence Behind Closed Doors", (1986) 136 N.L.J. 1191; S. S. M. Edwards and A. Halpern, "Protection for the Victim of Domestic Violence: Time for Radical Revision?", [1991] J.S.W.F.L. 94; C. A. Coleman and A. K. Bottomley, "Police Conceptions of Crime and 'No Crime'" (1976) 5 Crim. L.R. 344, 352.

4

2.5 Violent behaviour is recorded to some extent in civil court statistics relating to divorce proceedings[21] but for a variety of reasons, divorce statistics are unlikely to reveal the true level of violence underlying divorces.[22] There is some evidence that violence occurs in considerably more marriages which end in divorce than is reflected in the number of petitions containing allegations of violence. One research project found that 20% of all women petitioning for divorce used evidence of their husbands' violence to support a petition based on his behaviour and a further 20% claimed that there had been episodes of violence within their marriages although they chose to base their petitions on other evidence.[23] This finding that 20% of wives' petitions contained allegations of violence was very similar to the result of our own court record study carried out for our report on the Ground for Divorce, in which the corresponding figure was 22%.[24] As regards applications under the domestic violence legislation itself, in 1989 there were 21,418 injunctions granted under section 1 of the Domestic Violence and Matrimonial Proceedings Act 1976, of which 14,239 were non-molestation injunctions only and to which 5,870 had a power of arrest attached. Powers of arrest were also attached to 3,421 injunctions granted in matrimonial proceedings and 193 people were committed to prison.[25] There were also 1,738 other applications for injunctions under the inherent jurisdiction of the court in matrimonial causes.[26]

(c) Causes

2.6 There is no generally accepted explanation of the reasons for domestic violence and abuse, although a number of different theories have been put forward.[27] However, none of these alone satisfactorily explains why violence occurs in one family and not in another. Given the range of situations in which violence occurs and the variety of people involved, it would be surprising if there were a simple explanation.[28] We think, however, that the various theories put forward in the literature are of relevance in giving an additional perspective to the problem. It must always be emphasised that, whatever the causes of domestic violence, the law should be concerned with its consequences and in particular with the need to supply adequate protection for its victims. The law should also provide an affirmation that victims do not have to put up with violence, whatever the reason for its occurrence in the particular case.

2.7 Aspects of all these theories are controversial and leave parts of what is a very intricate problem unexplained. Also, other factors such as the use of drugs and alcohol may play a part, although they are not causes of domestic violence as such. The theories can be divided into three broad groups, outlined briefly below:

(i) Psychopathological theories

These theories argue that the violent person is ill or has an inadequate or defective personality, being typically aggressive, jealous and over possessive. Sometimes it is argued that the victim is masochistic or excessively dependent and insecure, or that the violence is a result of the interaction of two personalities with such traits. This has been developed to suggest that domestic violence is "learned behaviour" following a pattern copied from childhood experiences in a violent home and leading to cycles of violence in subsequent generations.[29]

(ii) Social and economic deprivation theories

These theories see domestic violence as a symptom of personal desperation, stress and frustration caused by blocked goals and problems such as financial difficulties, poor housing, unemployment, isolation or cultural differences.[30]

---

[21] In 1989, there were a total of 184,610 petitions for divorce, 89,050 (48%) of which were based on behaviour. Of these 76,590 (86%) were by wives. Lord Chancellor's Department, *Judicial Statistics*, Cm. 1154, (1989), Tables 5.2, 5.3. In 1990, a total of 191,615 petitions were issued but no breakdown of the different categories was published. Lord Chancellor's Department, *Judicial Statistics*, Cm. 1573, (1990), Table 5.1.

[22] S. Parker, "The legal background" in Pahl (ed.), *op. cit.*, p. 99.

[23] M. Borkowski, M. Murch and V. Walker, *Marital Violence: the Community Response*, (1983) p. 26.

[24] (1990) Law Com. No. 192, Appendix C. We found that 38.9% of petitions in our sample were based on behaviour, 91.8% of which were wives' petitions. Of these 64% contained allegations of violence committed by the husband.

[25] Judicial Statistics, *op. cit.*, Table 5.13.

[26] *Ibid.*, Table 5.9. However these figures may be unreliable as the relief sought is not specified and there are some unexplained discrepancies.

[27] Smith, *op. cit.*; Freeman, (1979), *op. cit.* pp. 21–32, 136–148; Clifton, *op. cit.*; M. D. A. Freeman, "Violence against women: does the legal system provide solutions or itself constitute the problem?", (1980) 7 Brit. J. Law and Soc. 215.

[28] The Australian Law Reform Commission, *op. cit.*, p. 11.

[29] Pizzey, *op. cit.*; J. J. Gayford, "Battered Wives", in Martin (ed.), (1975), *op. cit.*, p. 19.

[30] Discussion document of B.A.S.W. Working party on Home Violence (1975) 6 Social Work Today 409.

(iii) Theories about the position of women in society

These theories see domestic violence as having its roots in the very structure of the social and legal system. Although a husband's formal right to chastise his wife has long been abolished, it has left a legacy of unequal power relationships between the sexes.[31] Feminist theories thus see violence against women as typical rather than rare behaviour and as a manifestation of this endemic patriarchal bias and a reflection of the subordinate status of wives and mothers.[32]

Criminal and Civil Law

2.8 Domestic violence is not simply a legal problem which can be eradicated by the appropriate legal remedies. It is also a social and psychological problem which can be eliminated only by fundamental changes in society and in attitudes to women and children. While legal remedies are an attempt to alleviate the symptoms of domestic violence, they can do little to tackle the causes. Also, their effectiveness can be hampered by various factors.[33] First, they have to operate in an area where there is a constant tension between the need for instant protection to be given to the victim and the need to observe due process in the conduct of proceedings against the alleged perpetrator. A balance has to be struck between the victim's need and the rights of other people, although there is, of course, room for argument about what the correct balance should be.[34] Also, legal remedies can be undermined by the gap which exists between the letter and spirit of the law and the law in practice. It has been said that those who work in this area, including solicitors, barristers, police, court staff and judiciary, can, perhaps unconsciously, deter applicants from pursuing their proceedings or prevent the law operating as effectively as it might, if their reactions are affected by particular perceptions of male and female roles or an ambivalence about the propriety of legal or police intervention within the family.[35] As a recent study has concluded, "whatever legal reforms may be made, and whatever changes may be made to court procedures, without effective enforcement by police officers and by courts, injunctions and protection orders will continue to be 'not worth the paper they are written on'".[36]

2.9 Remedies against domestic violence are provided not only by family law, but also by criminal law and the law of tort. An incident of domestic violence will often amount to an assault or battery and to an offence against the person. But, although parts of the law of tort and the criminal law are specifically designed to deal with violence and the risk of harm (and have therefore developed useful machinery for this purpose such as arrest and remand), they remain blunt instruments in the context of domestic violence because of the relationship between the parties. Criminal law is primarily intended to punish the offender and actions in assault and battery to compensate the victim. However, most victims of domestic violence are not primarily interested in punishment or compensation. They want the violence to stop and they want protection.[37] Sometimes they want the relationship to end or at least be suspended, but sometimes they do not. The first aim of the civil domestic violence legislation should be to provide this protection in a flexible way which enables account to be taken of different victims' differing needs and of the many special considerations which apply in this area of the law. Thus, for example, many victims, particularly if they have children, will continue to live with the perpetrator or at least to maintain a relationship with him. They will often be financially and psychologically dependent upon him and there will be a high degree of emotional involvement making victims especially vulnerable to pressure or intimidation. Therefore the remedies provided should not cause any further deterioration in an ongoing relationship, and should be capable of regulating the parties' conduct in relationships which are breaking or have broken down. People from ethnic minorities may face additional difficulties. Cultural factors and racism can create special reasons for domestic violence, or special problems for those seeking to escape from it.[38]

---

[31] Freeman, *op. cit.*; Pahl, *op. cit.*, pp. 186–192; S. Maidment, "Domestic Violence and the Law: the 1976 Act and its aftermath", in Johnson (ed.), *op cit.*, (1985), p. 4.

[32] Women's Aid Federation England Ltd., *Breaking Through! Women surviving male violence*, (1989), pp. 57–63.

[33] See Women's National Commission, *Violence Against Women: report of an ad hoc working group*, (1985), para. 108.

[34] See para. 2.10 below.

[35] Edwards and Halpern, *op. cit.*, p. 97; Maidment, *op. cit.*, (1985); S. D. Migdal, "Domestic Violence: has the Act beaten it?" (1979) 9 Fam. Law 136; S. Maidment, "Laws for Battered Women—are they an improvement?, (1977) 7 Fam. Law 50; S. Parsloe, "Battered by men and bruised by the Law", Law Mag., 1987, September 4, 22.

[36] J. Barron, *Not Worth the Paper: the effectiveness of legal protection for women and children experiencing domestic violence*, (1990), p. 136.

[37] Dobash et al., *op. cit.*, pp. 146–163; C.R.A.W.C., *op. cit.*, p. 60.

[38] A. Mama, *The Hidden Struggle: statutory and voluntary sector responses to violence against black women in the home*, (1989).

2.10 The possible responses to domestic violence lie along a continuum at one end of which is the use of criminal penalties and at the other, referral to therapy or counselling. The two extremes reflect a philosophical difference of opinion upon the correct approach to the problem. On the one hand, there is the view that those who beat their partners should be treated just like any other criminal and should be routinely arrested and prosecuted.[39] Adopting any other approach is seen as giving the perpetrator the message that such behaviour is not really serious and is excusable, thus reinforcing the attitudes which led to the violence in the first place and implicitly condoning it. Some of our respondents were opposed to the idea of therapy or counselling being given to aggressors as they saw this as diverting resources from providing housing and assistance for the victims who are in much greater need. On the other hand, it can be argued that, particularly where the parties are still living together and the violence is a symptom of difficulties in a relationship rather than the cause, "automatic" prosecution can do more harm than good and may precipitate the final breakdown of the family. In some cases, a final separation may be the right course, but in others it may not. Imprisonment usually leads to loss of employment and to consequent financial hardship for the victim and children. It may exacerbate the problem by inciting further violence, and the children may suffer as a result of separation from their father. Unless the defendant has independent financial resources, fines or compensation are counter-productive as they simply reduce the finances available to maintain the family. It is not possible to say that either approach is the "correct" one. There is something to be said for both, and one is certainly likely to be more appropriate than the other in any particular case. As we have already explained, we are not in this report concerned with the sanctions available in the criminal law, although their existence and use are an important part of the context within which the civil law remedies may be used.

2.11 The civil domestic violence remedies approach the problems from a perspective which has a number of important differences from the approach of the criminal law.[40] The emphasis is more upon the needs of the victim: she can choose to apply for the remedy she wants. Although the remedies are discretionary, the facts have to be proved only upon the balance of probabilities and not beyond reasonable doubt and issues of intention and *mens rea* are not relevant. Civil remedies are prospective and positive: their main aim is to regulate and improve matters for the future, rather than to make judgments upon or punish past behaviour. Unlike criminal proceedings, they can also provide an immediate means of evicting the perpetrator from the home. This is often the only effective method of stopping abuse and molestation, as when the parties live together there are unique opportunities for it to continue. If the perpetrator is arrested and charged with a criminal offence, he will usually be released on bail, albeit with conditions regulating his conduct, until the trial. Unless there are serious injuries, he is likely to receive a non-custodial or fairly short sentence and be released, whereupon he is free to return home. These sanctions are, quite rightly, related to the comparative gravity of the offence (and the record of the offender) in the scale of offending as a whole. Although domestic cases are now taken much more seriously than they used to be by police, prosecutors and the courts, the consequences bear no relation to the future needs of the victim. In civil proceedings, on the other hand, it may be possible to obtain an immediate ouster order which can continue until she is able to take divorce proceedings and obtain a property transfer order or find alternative accommodation. Thus, although civil proceedings do not result in a criminal record, their practical consequences may sometimes be more serious for the respondent in other respects.

2.12 But, although civil proceedings have certain advantages, civil remedies are not in general designed to handle violence and other forms of extreme behaviour normally dealt with under the criminal law. To make the remedies properly effective for the purposes they are intended to serve within this particular context, it has been found necessary to develop certain specialised quasi-criminal machinery, principally powers of remand and arrest. Attaching a power of arrest to an injunction is a serious step as it places the respondent at risk of losing his liberty, at least for a short time without a court deciding that the respondent has breached the injunction. However, the power will often be the only effective means of deterring the respondent from a breach, or of protecting the victim should it occur. A large majority of our respondents who commented on this issue regarded powers of arrest as an

---

[39] Some American studies have shown that a policy of arrest by the police can substantially reduce new incidents of battery. L. W. Sherman and R. A. Berk, "The specific deterrent effect of arrest for domestic assault" (1984) 49 Am. Soc. Rev. 26; R. A. Berk and P. J. Newton, "Does arrest really deter wife battery? An effort to replicate the findings of the Minneapolis Spouse Abuse Experiment" (1985) 50 Am. Soc. Rev. 253.

[40] For a comparison see S. Maidment, "The Relevance of the Criminal Law to Domestic Violence", [1980] J.S.W.L. 26.

important resource in enforcing the law and favoured their extension beyond the circumstances in which they can be granted at present.[41]

2.13 Disputes about the occupation of the family home and applications for ouster or exclusion orders can arise in a variety of circumstances. In a common case, an ouster order may be sought to evict a man from the house where a non-molestation injunction is felt to be insufficient protection against his violence. Alternatively one party may be inflicting an intolerable degree of non-violent harassment upon the other, or there may be no particular violence or harassment, but the parties' relationship has broken down and the tensions and strains of living in the same house have become too great for them or their children to bear.

2.14 Different policy considerations may apply to cases where an ouster order is sought for protection and those in which it is sought to resolve disputes over the occupation of the home during or following relationship breakdown, although in practice the dividing line between them may be difficult to draw. The former needs a clear and urgent response, whereas in the latter immediate relief and protection are not required to secure personal safety, however desperate the applicant may be to live apart from her partner. There is often, however, a need for a practical solution to the family's problem for the sake of all concerned, particularly if there are children. There may also be a difference in the time span for which relief is needed. Short term relief may provide sufficient protection in some cases, simply by creating a breathing space to allow the applicant to find alternative accommodation or the respondent time to come to terms with the changed situation. But in cases where the relationship has permanently broken down, a medium term solution will often be needed until the question of occupation of the property can be permanently settled, usually by an application under section 24 of the Matrimonial Causes Act 1973 or under the ordinary law of property.[42] In a few cases, for example where a married couple do not want to divorce or to dispose of the property, a long term solution may be needed.

Housing law

(a) The homelessness legislation

2.15 Some of our respondents thought it essential to consider the question of occupation of the home in the context of wider issues of housing.[43] There is a serious national housing shortage and there has in recent years been a steady increase in the numbers of people accepted as homeless.[44] In these circumstances, it can be very hard either for a single person, particularly if unemployed, or for a single parent with children to obtain satisfactory affordable accommodation. Most people have few choices. Imposing on friends or relatives is generally only a short term possibility and usually means living in overcrowded conditions. Private landlords are frequently unwilling to accept tenants who are dependent on welfare benefits, making private rented accommodation difficult to find or afford. The main alternatives for women seeking to escape an intolerable situation are therefore to rely on the homelessness legislation or to go to a Women's Aid refuge.[45] The main alternative for men leaving or evicted from home may well be a bed-sit or a men's hostel.

2.16 Since 1977, local authorities have had statutory duties to provide help for people who are rendered homeless.[46] The extent of these duties varies according to whether the person concerned is intentionally homeless and whether or not he or she has a priority need. No-one is to be regarded as intentionally homeless if, because they are at risk of violence or threats of violence from some other person residing there, they leave accommodation in

---

[41] See paras. 5.11–5.14 below.

[42] Such as an application under the Law of Property Act 1925, s.30.

[43] A view shared by others, e.g. F. Logan, *Homelessness and Relationship Breakdown*, (1986).

[44] In 1989, local authorities in Great Britain accepted as homeless and found accommodation for 148,000 households, an increase of 8% on 1988. Of these, 134,000 households were in a priority need category, 11,000 more than in 1988 and 22,000 more than in 1986. This is against a background of a decline during the 1980s in the total stock of local authority and new town dwellings to the levels of 20 years ago, see O.P.C.S., *Social Trends 21*, (1991), pp. 136–140. During the 1980s, the stock of rented housing in London was reduced by nearly 300,000 and the private rented sector alone shrank by over 40%. Since 1979, council building has been cut by 85% and over 1.5 million council houses have been sold, see J. Greve, *Homelessness in Britain*, (1991).

[45] V. Binney, G. Harknell and J. Nixon, "Refuges and housing for battered women", in Pahl (ed.), (1985), *op. cit.*, p. 166.

[46] Housing (Homeless Persons) Act 1977, now Housing Act 1985, Part III. Under s.58, a person is homeless if there is no reasonable accommodation which he and his family are entitled to occupy in England, Wales and Scotland.

8

which they are entitled to live.[47] The criteria for being in priority need include being (a) a pregnant woman, (b) a person with whom dependent children reside or might reasonably be expected to reside, (c) vulnerable because of old age, disability or handicap or (d) homeless because of a natural disaster.[48] Housing authorities have a duty to provide suitable accommodation for homeless people with a priority need who are not intentionally homeless.[49] But, although many victims of domestic violence should qualify for this, problems can sometimes arise in practice[50] and waiting lists for council houses generally mean enduring many months in temporary bed and breakfast accommodation.

2.17 Housing authorities owe lesser duties to other homeless people. People with a priority need who became homeless intentionally are entitled only to temporary accommodation for such period as the authority considers will give them a reasonable opportunity of finding their own accommodation and to advice and assistance towards doing this.[51] Such people without a priority need are entitled only to advice and assistance,[52] which is probably of little practical value. A man evicted from his house under an exclusion or ouster order is most likely to fall into the latter category, although a single man without children, particularly if he is in employment, has a better chance than most of finding and affording alternative private accommodation.

(b) Public sector housing

2.18 Changes to the law introduced in the Housing Act 1980, gave council tenants security of tenure.[53] As a consequence of this they enjoy secure status and, short of a voluntary assignment or surrender, a local authority can only deprive a tenant of his security by bringing successful proceedings for possession against him.[54] Whilst this has brought many benefits from the tenants' point of view, it has also given rise to certain unforeseen difficulties, both for women with children and for local authorities in terms of regulating the occupation of a council house on the breakdown of a relationship.[55] Local authorities are now no longer able to resolve, by serving a notice to quit, the situation of a tenant occupying on his own a house intended for his family but from which his wife or cohabitant has fled with the children, often to present herself as homeless and in priority need.[56] The family law remedies available in respect of the family home may therefore be the only way of resolving the problems while preserving the security of the tenancy. This has increased both the involvement of the courts and the need for the available remedies to be effective, accessible and comprehensive.

2.19 Short term solutions may be available in the form of ouster or exclusion orders,[57] but frequently this will not be enough as once the ouster order expires, the man is entitled

---

[47] Housing Act 1985, s.58(3); there are also dicta to suggest that a woman who is at risk of violence or threats of violence from someone outside the home who nonetheless threatens her while she is in it is also eligible for assistance, R. v. Kensington and Chelsea Royal London Borough Council, ex parte Hammell [1989] Q.B. 578; R. v. Broxbourne Borough Council, ex parte Willmoth (1989) 20 H.L.R. 554. Also, the Code of Guidance which accompanies the Housing Act expressly states that a battered woman who has fled the marital home should never be regarded as having become homeless intentionally, para. 2:12.

[48] Housing Act 1985, s.59(1). The Code of Guidance states that local authorities should consider women without children to be "vulnerable" if they are at risk of violence, para. 2:12(c)(iii).

[49] Ibid., s.65(2).

[50] Some housing authorities refuse to treat a battered woman as being in priority need until she has obtained a custody order (despite dicta to the contrary, R. v. Ealing London Borough, ex parte Sidhu (1982) 80 L.G.R. 534) creating a "catch 22" situation where she cannot obtain a custody order because she does not have suitable accommodation and cannot obtain accommodation because she does not have a custody order. Other housing authorities may take the view that a woman who leaves home without first seeking non-molestation and exclusion injunctions has acted unreasonably and is therefore intentionally homeless. P. D. Reekie and R. Tuddenham, Family Law and Practice, (1990), pp. 442–443; Binney et al., op. cit., pp. 173–177. See also R. Thornton, "Homelessness Through Relationship Breakdown: The Local Authorities' Response", [1989] J.S.W.L. 67.

[51] Housing Act 1985, s.65(3).

[52] Ibid., s.65(4).

[53] ss.28(3) and 32, now Housing Act 1985, ss.81 and 82.

[54] Under one of the grounds laid down in the Housing Act 1985, Schedule 2, none of which is immediately relevant to cases of domestic violence or relationship breakdown.

[55] The Department of the Environment has set up an inter-departmental working party to look at the problems arising with the allocation of public sector housing on relationship breakdown. See generally, D. C. Hoath, Public Housing Law, (1989), pp. 248–269; D. Pearl, "Public Housing Allocation and Domestic Disputes", in M. D. A. Freeman (ed.), Essays in Family Law, (1985), p. 20; C. Williams, "Ouster Orders, Property Adjustment and Council Housing", [1988] Fam. Law 438.

[56] Thornton, op. cit., pp. 67–8; J. Bull and M. Stone, "When relationships break down", Housing, April 1991, p. 13.

[57] Ouster orders under the Domestic Violence and Matrimonial Proceedings Act 1976 are usually made for a maximum of 3 months in the first instance, see Practice Direction [1978] 1 W.L.R. 1123; Davis v. Johnson [1979] A.C. 26. The remedies available to cohabitants are more restricted than those available to spouses, see para. 2.28 below.

to return and exercise his right of occupation. The prospects of obtaining a lengthy ouster order are poor,[58] and even if it is obtained, the problem is simply postponed. In some cases, it may be impossible even to obtain a short term order, for example, where the parties are cohabitants who can no longer be said to be living with each other as husband and wife, the courts have no jurisdiction even to grant a short term ouster order under the Domestic Violence and Matrimonial Proceedings Act 1976, and a complete deadlock arises which neither the courts or the local authority can resolve.[59]

2.20 If the parties are married, long term solutions are available in the form of an order transferring the tenancy under section 7 of and Schedule 1 to the Matrimonial Homes Act 1983 or ancillary to divorce proceedings under section 24 of the Matrimonial Causes Act 1973. But there are no equivalent provisions for cohabitants. If the cohabitants are joint tenants it is possible for the woman to put an end to the tenancy by giving the council notice to quit, having agreed with them beforehand that they will regrant the tenancy to her alone.[60] However, this course could present a degree of risk as it means that the woman is dependent upon the good will of the local authority. There is also a chance that it may give rise to liability for breach of trust.[61] If the tenancy is in the man's sole name, there is no clear solution short of a voluntary surrender.[62]

Defects in the present remedies in family law

2.21 There are three different statutes giving the courts express powers to grant non-molestation orders or injunctions and to regulate the occupation of the family home by way of ouster, exclusion or other orders. The Domestic Violence and Matrimonial Proceedings Act 1976 empowers county courts to grant injunctions against molestation or exclude one party from the home, not only between spouses but also between men and women living together as husband and wife, and also to attach powers of arrest to certain injunctions however granted.[63] The Domestic Proceedings and Magistrates' Courts Act 1978 gives magistrates' courts power to make orders protecting one spouse from violence by the other, and in some cases to exclude one spouse from the home and to attach powers of arrest.[64] The Matrimonial Homes Act 1983 gives one spouse the right to occupy a matrimonial home to which the other is entitled, makes those rights a charge upon the estate or interest of the entitled spouse, and enables the High Court or a county court to enforce or restrict the respective rights of spouses to occupy the home.[65]

2.22 These statutory powers were superimposed on the existing general powers of the High Court and county courts to grant injunctions.[66] Such powers are ancillary to some other remedy within the court's jurisdiction, or in support of a right recognised by the general law. Thus, for many years divorce courts have granted injunctions against molestation or

---

[58] *Freeman* v. *Collins* (1983) 4 F.L.R. 649; Hoath, *op. cit.*, p. 259.

[59] *Ainsbury* v. *Millington* [1986] 1 All E.R. 73, where an unmarried couple with a baby were granted a joint tenancy of a council property. The respondent was imprisoned for burglary. Meanwhile the applicant married another man. On his release, the respondent returned home, forcing the applicant, her husband and child to move out. The Court of Appeal upheld the decision of the county court judge that he had no jurisdiction to oust the respondent from the premises so that the applicant could return.

[60] In *Greenwich L.B.C.* v. *McGrady* (1982) 6 H.L.R. 36, it was held that notice to quit by one joint tenant, without the prior knowledge or consent of the other, was enough to terminate the tenancy. This decision has recently been upheld by the House of Lords in *Hammersmith and Fulham L.B.C.* v. *Monk* [1991] 3 W.L.R. 1144.

[61] Where the parties are joint tenants, they hold the property as trustees (Law of Property Act 1925, s.36(1)). Thus it could be that terminating the tenancy without consent might amount to a breach of trust giving rise to a claim for substantial damages, particularly if it includes further loss under the "right to buy" provisions. If the woman persuades the local authority to regrant the tenancy to her alone, she may be in the position of a trustee who is attempting to benefit from her breach of trust and if so would hold the equitable estate on a constructive trust for both herself and the man concerned, making the entire process a complete waste of time. See further P. H. Pettit, *Equity and the Law of Trusts*, (6th ed.), (1989), p. 144. However, doubt has recently been cast on this interpretation on the ground that the overreaching statutory trusts for sale imposed by the Law of Property Act 1925 do not normally alter the beneficial rights inter se of the concurrent owners, *Hammersmith and Fulham L.B.C.* v. *Monk* [1991] 3 W.L.R. 1144, 1156 *per* Lord Browne-Wilkinson.

[62] Hoath, *op. cit.*, at pp. 268–269 suggests the possibility of the local authority putting pressure on a tenant to surrender the tenancy by legitimately increasing the rent in view of gross under-occupation, or the possibility of obtaining such a lengthy ouster order under the Domestic Violence and Matrimonial Proceedings Act 1976 that the excluded tenant no longer fulfils the condition of "occupying the dwelling as his only or principal home", and loses his security. However, it is difficult to obtain a lengthy ouster order and no guarantee that once obtained, it would necessarily have this effect.

[63] ss.1 and 2.

[64] s.16(2) and (3).

[65] ss.1(2) and 9(1).

[66] Supreme Court Act 1981, s.37; County Courts Act 1984, s.38.

even excluded a spouse from the matrimonial home in response to applications made ancillary to divorce, separation or nullity proceedings in order to enable the petitioner to pursue her action free from intimidation.[67] The High Court and county courts can also grant injunctions to protect victims from the torts of assault, battery, nuisance or trespass, or in support of any other unrecognised property right.[68]

2.23 There are many inconsistencies and anomalies in the present law. These have arisen largely as a result of piecemeal statutory development and the adoption or adaptation of a remedy developed for a particular purpose in one context for different purposes in another.[69] The existing remedies have been developed in response to a variety of needs. Those under the Matrimonial Homes Act 1983 were first introduced in 1967[70] in order to ensure that deserted wives were not left without a roof over their heads, by giving them rights of occupation in the matrimonial home which could be registered and enforced against third parties, and by giving the court power to regulate occupation of the matrimonial home in the long or short term. To this was later added a power to prohibit the exercise by the property-owning spouse of his right to occupy the home.[71] The remedies provided in sections 16–18 of the Domestic Proceedings and Magistrates' Courts Act 1978 and the Domestic Violence and Matrimonial Proceedings Act 1976 have protection against violence and molestation as their primary objective and were designed to provide an urgent legal response to this, which could include an exclusion order where the circumstances justified it. The principles applicable to regulating occupation of the home in the short or long term and to providing protection from violence and molestation are not necessarily the same. But it is impossible to treat them separately because, very often, the removal of one party from the house is the only effective protection which can be provided in cases of violence.

2.24 In the working paper, we reviewed the development of these various remedies[72] and their operation.[73] The fact that different remedies are available to different applicants on different criteria in different courts with different enforcement procedures has resulted in a vastly complicated system, made even more confusing by the complex inter-relationship between the statutory remedies and the general principles of property and tort law.[74] In the first place, the scope of orders available under the different Acts differ. For instance, orders under the Domestic Violence and Matrimonial Proceedings Act 1976 can be wider than those under the Matrimonial Homes Act 1983 in that they can be tailored to allow the respondent to return to the property for the purpose of, for example, visiting children or carrying on a business;[75] but at the same time they are narrower in that there is no power to make ancillary orders about the discharge of outgoings or payment for occupation.[76] Again, the Domestic Violence and Matrimonial Proceedings Act 1976 allows the exclusion of the respondent from an area around the family home,[77] whereas this is not possible under the Domestic Proceedings and Magistrates' Courts Act 1978 or the Matrimonial Homes Act 1983. Yet we understand that exclusion zone orders are frequently made by the courts in the context of matrimonial proceedings in which the principles in the 1983 Act are applied.

2.25 The criteria applicable under the different Acts are also diverse and, in many ways, unsatisfactory in themselves. Neither the general powers under which the Courts grant injunctions in pending proceedings or the 1976 Act lay down any criteria for the exercise of the court's discretion.[78] But, despite the fact that the courts had developed their own

---

[67] e.g. *Silverstone* v. *Silverstone* [1953] P. 174; *Hall* v. *Hall* [1971] 1 W.L.R. 404. See also working paper No. 113, *op. cit.*, paras. 2.2–2.3.

[68] See working paper No. 113, *op. cit.*, paras. 2.8–2.9 and, e.g. *Egan* v. *Egan* [1975] Ch. 218; *Tabone* v. *Seguna* [1986] 1 F.L.R. 591; *Smith* v. *Smith* [1988] 1 F.L.R. 179; *Patel* v. *Patel* [1988] 2 F.L.R. 179.

[69] In an international review of remedies for violence against women in the family, the United Nations has commented that "The scheme in England and Wales provided by three different pieces of legislation which apply to different relationships and in different circumstances and give different relief presents even experienced lawyers with difficulties", United Nations, *op. cit.*, p. 91, n.117.

[70] By the Matrimonial Homes Act 1967 at a time when it was more usual for matrimonial homes to be in the husband's sole name.

[71] Domestic Violence and Matrimonial Proceedings Act 1976, ss.3 and 4, reversing the effect of *Tarr* v. *Tarr* [1973] A.C.254.

[72] Working paper No. 113, paras. 2.1–2.16.

[73] *Ibid.*, paras. 3.1–3.18.

[74] See paras. 3.13–3.17 below.

[75] See also Domestic Proceedings and Magistrates' Courts Act 1978, s.16(9).

[76] Matrimonial Homes Act 1983, s.1(3)(b) and (c).

[77] Domestic Violence and Matrimonial Proceedings Act 1976, s.1(1)(c).

[78] Supreme Court Act 1981, s.37 and County Courts Act 1984, s.38 refer simply to what is "just and convenient".

principles to govern the exercise of this jurisdiction,[79] in *Richards* v. *Richards*,[80] the House of Lords decided that the criteria set out in section 1(3) of the 1983 Act[81] should be applied in any case where an ouster order is sought between spouses, whether under that Act, the 1976 Act or in pending matrimonial proceedings.[82] These criteria are not, however, applied in applications for exclusion orders under the Domestic Proceedings and Magistrates' Courts Act 1978. This Act has its own criteria based mainly on the use or threat of violence and danger of injury.[83]

2.26 A number of possible criticisms of the present law, and in particular the application of the Matrimonial Homes Act criteria, were put forward in the working paper[84] and were generally approved by those who responded to it. These can be summarised as follows:

(i) the criteria are now out-dated, having first been enacted in 1967[85] for the purpose of identifying those non-owning spouses (usually wives) who were sufficiently deserving of long term accommodation in the matrimonial home to entitle them to resist dispositions to third parties; this was before most of the significant developments in this field;[86]

(ii) by requiring the parties' conduct to be balanced against the other factors, the criteria may suggest that an ouster order is in effect punishment for bad behaviour, so that the court should be asking itself whether the respondent's conduct is serious enough to justify an order, rather than whether the effect upon the other people in the household is serious enough to do so;[87]

(iii) these criteria with their concentration upon the conduct of the parties are applied to the whole range of very different situations:[88] the need to provide immediate protection against violence or other forms of abuse; the need to resolve short term problems of accommodation when a relationship is or may be breaking down; and the need to resolve longer term problems where the relationship has already broken down;

(iv) where divorce proceedings have already begun, there may well be a need to resolve disputes about who should live in the matrimonial home in the short term, and if possible this should be done without either pre-judging issues which may be in dispute in the proceedings[89] or forcing upon the parties a procedure that is based on language relying on conduct and fault whether or not they wish to pursue the disputes between them in those terms;[90]

(v) there is a risk that the children's welfare will be given insufficient weight,[91] contrary to the general trend towards giving increased, if not predominating, weight to their interests even in relation to matters of finance and property;[92]

---

[79] Based mainly upon relative hardship to the parties and the interests of the children, see *Bassett* v. *Bassett* [1975] Fam. 76; *Walker* v. *Walker* [1978] 1 W.L.R. 533.

[80] [1984] A.C. 174.

[81] s.1(3) provides that "the court may make such order as it thinks just and reasonable having regard to the conduct of the spouses in relation to each other and otherwise, to their respective needs and financial resources, to the needs of any children and to all the circumstances of the case".

[82] The same criteria have also been extended to applications between cohabitants, despite the fact that the Matrimonial Homes Act 1983 does not apply to them; *Lee* v. *Lee* [1984] F.L.R. 243.

[83] Section 16(3); the respondent must have (i) used violence against the applicant or a child of the family, or (ii) threatened to use violence against the applicant or child and actually used it against someone else, or (iii) threatened to use violence against the applicant or a child in breach of a personal protection order; and the applicant or child must be in danger of being physically injured by the respondent.

[84] Working paper No. 113, paras. 3.19–3.25.

[85] When the law of divorce and other matrimonial remedies still largely depended upon proving a matrimonial offence.

[86] e.g. the Divorce Reform Act 1969, which replaced the doctrine of the matrimonial offence with that of irretrievable breakdown of the marriage; the Matrimonial Proceedings and Property Act 1970, which introduced powers of property adjustment on divorce; and the emergence both of concern about violence and other forms of abuse within the family during the 1970s and of the widespread phenomenon of cohabitation outside marriage during the 1980s.

[87] See, e.g. *Wiseman* v. *Simpson* [1988] 1 W.L.R. 35.

[88] See paras. 2.13 and 2.14 above.

[89] Whether in relation to the longer term occupation of the home or in relation to the allegations in the divorce petition: the course adopted by the Court of Appeal in *Baynham* v. *Baynham* [1968] 1 W.L.R. 1890 of making an interim exclusion order without a full trial of issues of conduct which would be decided in the pending divorce proceedings would not apparently be possible now.

[90] The policy of the law is summed up in the terms of reference of the Matrimonial Causes Procedure Committee (the Booth Committee), which was appointed in 1982 to recommend reforms which might be made: "(a) to mitigate the intensity of disputes; (b) to encourage settlements; and (c) to provide further for the welfare of the family".

[91] See e.g. *Summers* v. *Summers* [1986] 1 F.L.R. 343, C.A. where the judge had decided that it was not in the children's interests to witness continuing bitter quarrels between their parents, who were equally at fault but was held to have given this too much weight as against the Draconian nature of the order.

[92] Matrimonial Causes Act 1973, s.25(1), as substituted by Matrimonial and Family Proceedings Act 1984, s.3.

(vi) a general assumption that the effects of an exclusion order are invariably so severe as to merit the terms drastic or even Draconian, while obviously warranted in many cases,[93] may obscure the considerable differences between the circumstances of the individual parties[94] and in which the remedy is sought;[95] in combination with a requirement that the respondent's conduct be bad enough to merit such a step, this may impede the sensible and practical resolution of the particular problem presented;

(vii) the Matrimonial Homes Act criteria are not easily applicable to unmarried couples, for example because they do not give any indication of the relevance, if any, of respective property rights.

2.27 A further difficulty is that the present remedies available in the magistrates' courts are much more limited than those in the superior courts. The Domestic Proceedings and Magistrates' Courts Act 1978 applies only to spouses, not to cohabitants, and the remedies it provides are limited to cases of actual or threatened violence. There is thus no remedy in the magistrates' court for non-violent harassment.

2.28 The present law can also be criticised on the ground that it provides no protection for a number of people who have the misfortune to fall outside the specific categories of people covered by the different Acts, but may nevertheless have a clear need for such protection. Thus, many remedies are unavailable once the spouses are divorced. A former spouse cannot apply to a magistrates' court under the 1978 Act, nor can she apply under the 1976 Act unless she and her former husband are still living together as husband and wife after the decree.[96] Rights of occupation under the Matrimonial Homes Act 1983 also end on decree absolute unless the court has ordered otherwise.[97] Although it may be possible to obtain a non-molestation order and perhaps an ouster order in the divorce proceedings, there is no general power to adjust the parties' rights of occupation pending the conclusion of the ancillary relief application, and because the parties are no longer husband and wife, the court cannot attach a power of arrest to injunctions against violence under section 2 of the Domestic Violence and Matrimonial Proceedings Act 1976.[98] Similarly, in the case of cohabitants, there is no power to provide protection once the relationship has ended. The only alternative is to proceed in tort, but this is a more cumbersome procedure, and is unlikely to be as effective because of difficulties over the precise scope of the protection available against molestation.[99] Yet protection is often very necessary against former cohabitants or spouses who find it impossible to accept that the relationship is over.

2.29 A further serious limitation of the present law is the lack of any simple machinery comparable to that under the Matrimonial Homes Act for adjusting cohabitants' rights of occupation, or for determining claims to a beneficial interest in a property to which only one is legally entitled, such as that under section 17 of the Married Women's Property Act 1882 for married couples or engaged couples whose engagement is terminated.[100] For joint owners, the only course is an application for sale under section 30 of the Law of Property Act 1925, which may take some time. Also, as we have already seen, if the cohabitants are joint tenants of rented property there is no special machinery for resolving disputes between them and if the tenancy is secure, the landlord has no power to transfer it.[101]

2.30 Those who responded to the working paper were in broad agreement with us about the defects of and problems with the present law and, as we have previously said,[102] all the respondents who commented were in favour of the introduction of a new code containing a single, consistent set of remedies. This was generally considered to be the only effective

---

[93] Where, e.g. the premises have been the couple's home for a long time, the respondent is deeply attached to it, and will have serious difficulty in finding alternative accommodation, because he has limited resources and as a single homeless person will not have a priority need; see para. 2.17 above.

[94] Where, e.g. the respondent has recently arrived or has not regarded the premises as his permanent home, where he has suitable alternative accommodation already available to him, or where he has the resources readily to arrange it.

[95] e.g. at the beginning, or in the middle, or at the end of the breakdown of a long, medium or short term relationship, with or without children of that or an earlier one.

[96] s.1(2).

[97] ss.1(10) and 2(4).

[98] See further working paper No. 113, paras. 4.2–4.6.

[99] See para. 3.14 below.

[100] Law Reform (Miscellaneous Provisions) Act 1970, s.2(2).

[101] See paras. 2.18 and 2.20 above.

[102] See para. 1.3 above.

way of removing all the anomalies and inconsistencies of the existing law. Whilst agreeing with our basic aim of not reducing the level of protection at present available, many respondents were keen that we should take this opportunity to improve it in some respects. In particular, a substantial proportion of respondents felt that any reform should take account of the fact that domestic violence is not limited to violence between spouses, cohabiting partners and children, but is prevalent in many other forms of relationship.

Which basic approach to reform?

2.31 In the working paper, we suggested that there should be two different kinds of order, a non-molestation order and an occupation order, each with its own criteria and limitations.[103] Although few of our respondents commented directly upon this structure, it appeared to meet with general approval. However, this is not the only possible approach. There are other potential structures with different types of order and different criteria. Some of those who responded to our working paper put forward detailed alternative schemes of considerable attraction.

(a) An automatic truce

2.32 The Council of Her Majesty's Circuit Judges, in their response to the working paper, proposed a scheme which they thought would obviate the need for the courts to make non-molestation orders in many cases.[104] They argued that domestic violence needs to be considered in the context of the future relationships of the family as a whole and that the aim of any legislation should be to maximise opportunities for reconciliation and conciliation.[105] Hence, civil remedies should not be concerned with apportioning fault and encouraging parties to make allegations of misconduct, but should instead direct them towards a civilised adjustment and a constructive resolution of their problems.

2.33 The Circuit Judges therefore suggested that, upon a spouse or cohabitant making an application to the court in relation to the breakdown of their relationship, an automatic injunctive direction should be applied, forbidding each of the parties to use violence or molest the other or any child, to destroy or dissipate any family assets, to use any force or other molestation to gain care of or contact with any child or to remove the other party from the family home. This injunction would remain in force while proceedings were pending unless superseded by an order of the court or by mutual undertakings given to the court. Exclusion or ouster from the family home and powers of arrest would be available only when the court was of the opinion that the evidence showed, first that the automatic injunction was insufficient to protect the applicant, or any child of either party and, secondly that no child of the family would be unreasonably affected by such an order. It was also proposed that, whether or not automatic injunctions were introduced, whenever both parties attended on an inter partes application, they should be invited by the court to resolve their differences, as far as possible, by mutual undertakings. These proposals were based on the law or practice in a number of States in America, including New York and California,[106] where "mutual orders of protection" became the norm in the late 1970s and early 1980s, often as a result of judicial initiative.[107]

2.34 This scheme has many attractive features, particularly its attempt to reduce hostility and the bitterness which use of the present domestic violence remedies is thought to engender, especially where the violence or molestation has arisen as a symptom of the family breakdown, rather than its cause. However, it also gives rise to a number of practical and theoretical difficulties.

---

[103] Working paper No. 113, paras. 6.48, 6.60–6.63.

[104] Their response was published as Family and Civil Committees of the council of H.M. Circuit Judges, "Domestic Violence and Occupation of the Matrimonial Home", (1990) 20 Fam. Law 225.

[105] These are distinct concepts. Reconciliation is an outcome whereas conciliation is a process. Attempts at reconciliation are aimed at restoring a couple's relationship with a view to reuniting them. Conciliation, now commonly referred to as mediation, is a way of assisting separating or divorcing couples to reduce areas of conflict and resolve their disagreements without resort to conventional adjudication. It aims to help couples reach their own agreements, to improve communication between them and help them co-operate in the future over matters such as the upbringing of their children.

[106] Legislation has now been passed in California to provide that, with effect from 1 July 1990, summonses issued in family law proceedings should automatically contain standard restraining orders prohibiting the disposal of property without consent, changing insurance beneficiaries or coverage, removing minor children from the state and harassment and molestation. Californian Code of Civil Procedure, section 412.21 (as enacted by Stats. 1989, chap. 1105).

[107] Various aspects of how these orders operate in the United States are discussed by Peter Finn, "Statutory Authority in the Use and Enforcement of Civil Protection Orders Against Domestic Abuse", (1989) 23 F.L.Q. 43.

2.35 First, there is the fundamental difficulty that an injunction is a coercive order which not only has derogatory implications for those against whom it is made, but also puts them under threat of penal sanctions. We do not think it in principle acceptable for such an order to be issued automatically in the general run of family proceedings.

2.36 Secondly, the basic thrust of the proposals is misconceived in the context of domestic violence. Whilst it is possible to argue that automatic injunctions would be appropriate as part of matrimonial ancillary proceedings,[108] they do not deal effectively with incidents of domestic violence which are not associated with such proceedings. Mutual injunctions run contrary to the objective of domestic violence remedies, which is to provide immediate protection from violence in whatever context it occurs. If an applicant arrives at court complaining that she (or her child) has been the victim of serious violence, it will appear inappropriate and unjust for the court's standard reaction to be to impose orders, without further investigation, against both parties. We also doubt whether such orders will provide the necessary protection. Experience from New York State suggests that they have given rise to a number of problems.[109] First, family court judges might enter mutual orders of protection in family offence proceedings upon the oral request of the respondent or of their own motion without prior notice to the petitioner, and without any opportunity for testimony in rebuttal by the petitioner. If orders were made without investigation of the facts of the case, the petitioner might be seen as equally at fault. Secondly, such orders reinforce the erroneous belief that victims of domestic violence are partly responsible for their partners' violence and are active participants in it. Finally, these orders have been found to give the police an ambiguous direction as to enforcement, with the result that they tended to do nothing when summoned to the scene of an assault because they saw arresting both parties as the only alternative.

2.37 There are also a number of practical reasons for questioning the wisdom of imposing automatic mutual injunctions each time family proceedings are issued. Domestic injunctions form a high proportion of the workload of some circuit judges, but in reality the question of their issue only arises in a small proportion of all family cases. In the great majority of matrimonial proceedings, such injunctions would be completely unnecessary, and, it might not unreasonably be assumed, equally unwanted. It could well be regarded as heavy handed and disparaging to apply injunctions to people who have no disposition to be violent towards or to harass their partners or former partners, and will never actually do so. There may also be a risk that familiarity will breed contempt and that the use of injunctions in every case will reduce their impact when they really are needed.

2.38 It is also unclear how the automatic injunctions scheme would operate at the enforcement stage. When a respondent breaches a normal injunction, the court is generally able to start from the premise that he has previously committed the conduct he is now accused of repeating[110] or, in the case of a *quia timet* injunction, has sufficiently clearly threatened that conduct for the court to have been justified in enjoining him. However, with automatic injunctions, this assumption cannot apply. Thus, although, strictly speaking, the only relevant questions at the enforcement stage are whether the injunction was served, or came otherwise to the notice of the respondent, and whether the respondent then acted in breach of the injunction, the applicant will probably wish to prove her allegations about events which happened before the automatic injunctions were imposed, as well as events which occurred in breach of them, in order to justify her application for committal. This could cause the court to hold a trial of conduct and to allow any accompanying bitterness and recriminations to be aired. In that event such trial would simply take place later, rather than earlier, thus depriving the scheme of many of its possible benefits. Further, in order to enforce an injunction, proof of personal service is generally required.[111] Personal service of an automatic injunction is unlikely to improve relations between the parties, particularly if they are living under the same roof.

---

[108] See para. 2.33 above; although not, in our view, convincingly, see para. 2.40 below.

[109] Criticisms of these orders are voiced in the Report of the New York Task Force on Women in the Courts 1986, (1986–7) 25 Fordham Urban L.J. 11. The Task Force was established to "examine the courts and identify gender bias and, if found, make recommendations for its alleviation" (p. 16). It consisted of a panel of distinguished citizens from different backgrounds and its report was the culmination of a twenty-two month investigation undertaken on behalf of and under the auspices of the Unified Court System of the State of New York.

[110] For a non-molestation order to be granted there has to be some evidence of molestation having taken place, *Spindlow* v. *Spindlow* [1979] Fam. 52.

[111] Although an order requiring a person to abstain from doing something may be enforced even if service has not been personally effected, provided he has notice of it. R.S.C. O. 45, r. 7(6); C.C.R. O. 29, r. 1(6). See also *Husson* v. *Husson* [1962] 1 W.L.R. 1434.

2.39 There are also problems with the routine use of mutual undertakings. It has been said that "... they are often regarded with derision by the men and with resentment by the women ...".[112] Concern has also been expressed that encouraging parties to use undertakings as a first step both rides over the feelings of the applicants (that they are being inveigled into making inappropriate concessions) and ignores the stress and time involved in repeated visits to the solicitor and the court.[113] In addition, it is not, of course, possible to attach a power of arrest to an undertaking. It may well be that an invitation to the parties to give mutual undertakings is inappropriate unless there is actual reason to think that both parties have misbehaved and are likely to continue to do so.

2.40 Although this scheme may appear more appropriate in the context of divorce proceedings,[114] it nevertheless sits uneasily in a number of respects with our proposals to reform the ground for divorce.[115] Although both aim to be conciliatory, it is possible that the imposition of automatic injunctions or even the requirement of mutual undertakings would have the opposite effect. By inducing an automatic "stand-off", and instantly converting the spouses into adversaries, such injunctions might increase, rather than decrease, hostility and resentment. They would certainly impede some important objectives of the proposed waiting period, which are for the parties to reflect upon whether or not their relationship has indeed broken down irretrievably, to co-operate in seeking solutions for the future, and in particular to maintain communication with and about their children. It would seem likely that the imposition of mutual injunctions would reduce the effectiveness of this period as it would impede rather than assist communication, might well generate bitterness and animosity between the parties and hinder any attempt at conciliation or mediation.

2.41 The fundamental problem with this scheme is that its object is to avoid exacerbating relationships in matrimonial proceedings in general and not specifically to respond to domestic violence. Whilst it is arguably too heavy handed for the general run of matrimonial proceedings, it equally provides too lightweight a reaction to cases of violence which merit a more immediate and emphatic legal response. Overall, it seems that the disadvantages of the scheme are likely to outweigh its advantages.

(b) Short term and long term orders

2.42 The second limb of the proposals made by the Council of Her Majesty's Circuit Judges centred upon the duration for which orders are needed, and drew a distinction between Short Term Protection orders and Long Term Readjustment orders although both would be capable of dealing with occupation of the home, use of personal property, where children should live and who should have contact with them. Applications for non-molestation and exclusion injunctions following violence and molestation would normally be dealt with by a Short Term Protection order,[116] although they could exceptionally be dealt with in a Long Term Readjustment order. A Long Term Readjustment order would normally deal with rights of occupation as between the parties and provide for the rights of the parties vis-a-vis third parties such as mortgagees and landlords. The criteria for the two orders would differ. The main criterion for a Short Term Protection order would be protection from harm, probably (in view of the need to spare children from turmoil and violence between their parents) with the needs of children being paramount. The criteria for a Long Term Readjustment order would be the needs of the various family members along the lines of the "balance of hardship test" suggested in the working paper.[117]

2.43 These proposals were presented with the aim of reducing the need for court hearings, in the hope of sparing the parties distress and of saving legal costs and court time. In addition, they have the merit of providing for the very different situations in which ouster or exclusion orders may be sought.[118] However, valuable though the proposals are in these respects, there are difficulties with this structure. The distinction between short term and long term remedies certainly arises in practice, in that some types of remedy are often granted until a fixed return date. But this distinction does not always correspond to the

---

[112] Barron, *op. cit.*, p. 111.

[113] *Ibid.*, p. 111.

[114] See para. 2.36 above.

[115] *The Ground for Divorce*, (1990), Law Com. No. 192.

[116] If mutual undertakings or automatic injunctions are considered insufficient; see para. 2.33 above.

[117] See working paper No. 113, para. 6.62 and paras. 4.25 and 4.26 below.

[118] Failure to do which is one of the criticisms which can be made of the present system, see paras. 2.13, 2.14 and 2.26 above.

requirements of particular categories of applicant and is not therefore a justification for requiring the courts to distinguish between short term and long term orders in every case. Sometimes the need for a long term order may be apparent at the outset. Often, having solved the immediate problem, the parties do not need to return. It is also difficult to see why the criteria applied by the court should differ simply because of the duration, as opposed to the nature, of the remedy. In principle, the criteria upon which a decision is based should be appropriate to the nature of the remedy sought: the duration of the remedy is simply a matter of judgment according to the circumstances of the particular case. There must be a danger that the overall result of a two-tier system would be duplication and perhaps some confusion about the circumstance in which the different orders were appropriate.

(c) Singling out violence

2.44 Another model[119] would distinguish between cases where there has been actual or threatened physical violence, in which priority should be given to affording the victim proper protection, and cases where an ouster or exclusion order is sought in the context of the breakdown of a relationship, in which the need is to provide sensible and practical solutions to the transitional problems which arise. In the former, ouster and non-molestation orders would be granted virtually automatically or there would at least be a strong presumption in their favour. In the latter, if there are children and the parties cannot agree, the court would first decide with whom the children are to live and make a residence order. The court would then decide which partner should stay in the house and which should leave. The second decision would focus solely on the needs and resources of the parties, giving paramount consideration to the welfare of the children. If there are no children, the issue would be resolved simply on the balance of the partners' needs and resources. The court would fix a date upon which one partner should leave, allowing a breathing space to find alternative accommodation.

2.45 There are two main advantages to this model. First, by providing for an automatic or almost automatic ouster order in cases of violence, the law would make a strong statement against violence and give the best possible protection to victims. Secondly, it meets one of the criticisms of the present law[120] by enabling those whose relationships are breaking down to determine the occupation of the family home without trials of conduct.

2.46 Nevertheless, the scheme also has significant drawbacks. First, it is unclear where cases of harassment or abuse other than physical violence would fit into the scheme. By singling out violence, there is an implication that other forms of molestation are less serious, yet this will not always be so, for example, when a husband or cohabitant is sexually abusing children in the family. There are degrees of seriousness in all types of molestation, including violence, and it cannot necessarily be assumed that all cases of violence (or even child abuse) are more serious than all other cases. Consultation generally confirmed that, it would be undesirable to have less efficient remedies available against other forms of molestation than are available in cases of violence. Secondly, this scheme provides applicants with a strong incentive to allege (or even provoke) violence to make sure that they obtain an order. It may also encourage the courts to decide that violence has taken place, simply in order to achieve a sensible and practical resolution to the inevitable problems which arise when a relationship is breaking down. This can and does exacerbate hostilities between the parties. More importantly, it increases the attention paid to the seriousness (or otherwise) of the respondent's behaviour, rather than the needs of the parties and the effect on their children. Finally, a requirement that the court should first resolve the question of where the children should live might cause harmful delay. It may also run counter to the provision in the Children Act 1989 that the court should only make residence and other orders where this will be better for the child than making no order at all;[121] this will not necessarily be the case even where injunctions are being sought. The case for singling out violence is, we believe, much stronger in the area of enforcement, specifically powers of arrest, where it provides a clear justification for the involvement of the police in enforcing the orders of a civil court.

---

[119] Put forward principally by Mary Hayes J.P., Reader in Law at Sheffield University and a member of the Sheffield Family Proceedings Panel. The substance of her response was published as "The Law Commission and the Family Home" (1990) 53 M.L.R. 222.

[120] See para. 2.26 above.

[121] Children Act 1989, s.1(5).

(d) Conclusion

2.47 We have already indicated[122] that we consider that the disadvantages of any scheme for automatic injunctions or mutual undertakings outweigh the advantages. Nor do we think it either right in principle or necessary in practice for the law to distinguish between short and long term remedies or between violence and other forms of molestation or abuse. In practice, in any system of discretionary remedies, the court can distinguish between what is necessary or desirable in order to provide protection for the applicant and children in the short term and what is necessary or desirable to regulate the family's affairs in the medium term while decisions about divorce, reconciliation or indefinite separation are yet to be made. The court can also identify and react appropriately to cases involving serious violence. It does not need a statutory scheme to ensure that this takes place. The criteria can still be framed so as to ensure that these matters are relevant to the court's decision, without making them decisive in every case.

2.48 In principle, there must be a distinction between an order not to be violent towards or molest another family member, which can be obeyed without prejudice to the interests of the person concerned, and an order to leave or stay away from the home (or part of it), which obviously does prejudice those interests, however temporarily or justifiably. The present law is based on this distinction and does not present any problems in this respect. In view of the support given to the basic approach adopted in the working paper, and of the potential drawbacks of the alternatives, we have concluded that there is insufficient justification for changing that basic approach. We therefore *recommend* that the new scheme should provide for two distinct kinds of remedy, a non-molestation order and an occupation order, each with its own criteria and incidents but capable of combination with one another and with other family law remedies in an appropriate case.

---

[122] See para. 2.41 above.

18

PART III

NON-MOLESTATION ORDERS

Scope

3.1 Molestation is an umbrella term which covers a wide range of behaviour.[1] Although there is no statutory definition of molestation, the concept is well established and recognised by the courts. Molestation includes, but is wider than violence.[2] It encompasses any form of serious pestering or harassment[3] and applies to any conduct which could properly be regarded as such a degree of harassment as to call for the intervention of the court.[4] To obtain a non-molestation order, there has to be some evidence of molestation.[5] In the working paper[6] we asked whether the term "molestation" should be defined by statute. The overwhelming view of respondents was that any reform of the law in this area should not reduce the current level of protection from molestation. There was no evidence of problems having been caused in practice by lack of a statutory definition. Some concern was expressed that a definition might become over restrictive or that it could lead to borderline disputes. Consequently, we *recommend* that the courts should continue to have power to grant protection against all forms of molestation, including violence, and we further *recommend* that there should be no statutory definition of molestation.

3.2 Under the present law, the precise scope of a non-molestation injunction can be tailored to the requirements of the particular case. Traditionally, a common form of order restrains the respondent from "assaulting, molesting, or otherwise interfering" with the applicant. This general prohibition can be followed by a more precise injunction against specific kinds of behaviour complained of. It is important that non-molestation orders should retain this dual capability. Where it is obvious that there should be a limitation on a particular sort of behaviour, the order should be specific so that the respondent is left in no doubt about what he must stop doing. However, the order also needs to be sufficiently general to cover any other objectionable behaviour in which the respondent may subsequently decide to indulge.[7] Although the Civil Justice Review[8] recommended the use of standard forms for civil proceedings, standard forms of injunction can mean that some prohibitions which are included are inappropriate.[9] It seems to us that rigid standard forms and an even more rigid use of these are undesirable.[10] We therefore *recommend* that the power to make non-molestation orders be so framed as to make it clear that the order is a flexible one, capable of being tailored to the requirements of the particular case, but the court should also be able to prohibit molestation in its general form if the case so demands.

Criteria

3.3 In the working paper we asked whether the criteria for non-molestation orders should be defined.[11] The responses we received suggested that there are three possible approaches to this issue:

---

[1] See para. 2.3 above.

[2] "Violence is a form of molestation but molestation may take place without the threat or use of violence and still be serious and inimical to mental or physical health", *Davis* v. *Johnson* [1979] A.C. 264, 334 *per* Viscount Dilhorne.

[3] *Vaughan* v. *Vaughan* [1973] 1 W.L.R. 1159, 1162 where the respondent was calling at the plaintiff's house in the early morning and late at night and following her to her place of work when he knew that she was frightened of him.

[4] *Horner* v. *Horner* [1982] Fam. 90, in which it was held that handing the plaintiff menacing letters and intercepting her on her way to work amounted to molestation. See also *Johnson* v. *Walton* [1990] 1 F.L.R. 350 in which sending partially nude photographs of the plaintiff to a national newspaper for publication with the intent of causing her distress was held to come within a prohibition against molestation.

[5] *Spindlow* v. *Spindlow* [1979] Fam. 52.

[6] Working paper No. 113, paras. 6.15–6.16.

[7] The practice of the Courts in relation to injunctions against passing off is similarly not only to prohibit the particular conduct complained of but also to prohibit other modes of passing off. See, for example, the relief sought and granted in *Reckitt & Colman* v. *Borden Inc.* [1990] 1 W.L.R. 491.

[8] Lord Chancellor's Department, *Civil Justice Review: Report of the Review Body on Civil Justice*, Cm. 394, (1988).

[9] For example, at the moment it is common practice to include in non-molestation orders a provision that the respondent shall not communicate with the applicant in any way except through the applicant's solicitor. This may or may not be appropriate, particularly if there are children about whom arrangements have to be made.

[10] This is not necessarily incompatible with the sort of common sense, plain English forms suggested by Judge Fricker Q.C. and His Honour Douglas Forrester-Paton Q.C., [1988] Fam. Law 345. The present rules are contained in the County Court (Amendment) Rules 1991 and the County Court (Forms) (Amendment) Rules 1991; see also [1991] Fam. Law 148.

[11] Para. 6.26.

(i) to define the criteria quite precisely, perhaps singling out the use or threat of violence, as is the situation in the magistrates' courts at present;[12]

(ii) to leave them undefined, as they are in the higher courts as present; or

(iii) to adopt a broad statutory criterion, protecting the health, safety or well-being of the applicant or any child concerned, along the lines proposed in the working paper.

3.4 The purpose behind the first option was to secure a swift and virtually automatic response which would concentrate upon the victim's immediate need for protection and help to avoid the trivialisation of violence which can take place at present. However, as we have already suggested, there are significant disadvantages with this model.[13] In short, it places a premium upon alleging violence, it does not deal satisfactorily with cases of serious harassment and runs the risk of introducing an undesirable distinction between the levels of protection available against violence and other serious forms of molestation.

3.5 Responses to the working paper were equally divided between those who favoured having no statutory criterion and those who supported the working paper's suggestion[14] that the court should make such order as in all the circumstances is fair, just and reasonable in the interests of the health, safety or well-being of the applicant or any child concerned.[15] Support for leaving the criteria undefined was based on the fact that there is no evidence that the present discretion fails to provide a reasonable basis for the exercise of the jurisdiction. However, other respondents were in favour of defining criteria as it would promote consistency and it would make it clear that a non-molestation order could be obtained without the need to show physical violence.

3.6 The model proposed in the working paper seems to us to provide an acceptable degree of flexibility, bearing in mind that most forms of molestation are prohibited by the general law, so that the respondent's interests will rarely be seriously prejudiced by the order. A significant advantage is that it focuses the attention of the court upon the applicant's need for protection, and enables it to respond flexibly. One of the problems with singling out violence is that the response of the court would be dictated by the nature of the defendant's behaviour, rather than the effect upon the applicant or child concerned. In our preferred model, the nature of the defendant's behaviour is only relevant as far as its effect upon the applicant's health, safety and well-being, or that of any children involved, is concerned and this seems more appropriate, given both the purpose of this jurisdiction and the general trend in family law towards providing protection from harm rather than punishment or blame. In addition, it is important to emphasise that providing a statutory criterion will not restrict the definition of molestation. One aim of this project is to provide a complete and comprehensive code which is to be applied by all courts, including the magistrates' courts. The criteria we have suggested will promote consistency and give magistrates some help and guidance in exercising their powers under this new code.

3.7 We therefore *recommend* that the court should have power to grant a non-molestation order where this is just and reasonable having regard to all the circumstances including the need to secure the health, safety or well-being of the applicant or a relevant child.

Those who may be protected

(a) Parties

3.8 We originally suggested in the working paper that non-molestation orders should be available to protect spouses, former spouses, cohabitants, former cohabitants and perhaps parents or those with parental responsibility,[16] and certain children.[17] But although domestic violence tends to be thought of as taking place in a "husband and wife" context, there is no doubt that harassment and violence can occur in many types of relationship. For example, abuse of the elderly by members of the family with whom they are living is coming

---

[12] Domestic Proceedings and Magistrates' Courts Act 1978, s.16(2).

[13] See the analysis of this approach in paras. 2.44–2.46 above.

[14] At paras. 6.26 and 6.61.

[15] This is similar to the criterion thought by Lord Scarman to be appropriate for non-molestation orders under the 1976 Act in *Richards* v. *Richards* [1984] A.C. 174, 208.

[16] Defined in the Children Act 1989, s.3.

[17] Working paper No. 113, paras. 6.56 and 6.59.

increasingly to be recognised as a social problem[18] and significant numbers of women find it difficult or impossible to obtain protection from their violent teenage or adult sons.[19] The Council of Her Majesty's Circuit Judges has stressed to us that instances of family violence by adolescent sons and against elderly people by members of their family have become quite common. In the light of the representations we have received, we now consider that there is a case for extending the range of applicants eligible for this protection. There is an argument for having no limitations at all, on the basis that it is difficult to see why there should be any restrictions on the ground of relationship or residence if the main aim of the legislation is to provide protection from violence or molestation for people who need it. Why should applicants have to prove the existence of facts which do not relate directly to their need for protection if orders are only available on the ground that they are necessary for this purpose? On the other hand, to remove all restrictions would involve the creation of something approaching a new tort of harassment or molestation. The experience of other jurisdictions may be of some help here.

3.9 There is a variety of examples. The Australian states have all had new legislation in this area within the past decade. In New South Wales, the range of applicants is unlimited.[20] Since 1989, it has been possible for anyone to apply for an "apprehended violence order", essentially a civil injunction which covers behaviour amounting to any personal violence offence[21] and any harassment or molestation sufficient to warrant the making of an order.[22] Before 1989, this remedy was limited to "domestic" relationships,[23] but now there are no prescribed relationships, and it is available against anyone regardless of their connection with the applicant. It can therefore be sought against people such as neighbours, colleagues in the work place and acquaintances in respect of a wide range of annoying or intimidating conduct which is in itself beyond the reach of the criminal law or the law of tort. New South Wales also provides special criminal sanctions for "domestic violence offences". These retain the definition of "domestic" used before 1989 for the civil remedies and cover conduct amounting to a personal violence offence committed against a spouse, former spouse, cohabitant, former cohabitant, a person who is living or has lived ordinarily in the same household as the person who commits the offence (other than a tenant or a boarder), relatives, former relatives and a person who has had an intimate personal relationship with the person who commits the offence.[24] These sanctions are not available in cases of non-violent harassment or molestation, but in cases of violence where the parties come within the prescribed relationships, they have certain advantages over both a civil protection order and the ordinary criminal law.[25]

3.10 In Victoria, intervention orders may be made to protect "aggrieved family members". This term covers a spouse (including a former spouse and a de facto spouse), a relative or former relative of the violent person, a child of that person or a child of the spouse of that person or another person who is or has been ordinarily a member of the household of that person.[26] Unlike the New South Wales legislation, this does not expressly exclude people residing merely as tenants or boarders, but does not extend to the boyfriend or girlfriend of the violent party where there has been no cohabitation.[27]

---

[18] See J. Pritchard, "Confronting the taboo of the abuse of elderly people", Social Work Today, 5 October 1990, p. 22; M. D. A. Freeman, "The Abuse of the Elderly—Legal Responses in England", in J. Eekelaar and D. Pearl (eds.), *An Aging World: Dilemmas and Challenges for Law and Social Policy*, (1989), p. 741; P. Neate, "Home Truths", Community Care, 13 June 1991; S. Tomlin, *Abuse of Elderly People; an unnecessary and preventable problem*, (1989), The British Geriatric Society.

[19] Barron, *op. cit.*, p. 122.

[20] As it is in South Australia, (Justices Act 1921, as amended by the Justices Act Amendment (No. 2) 1982), Western Australia (Justices Act 1902, s.172 as amended by the Justices Amendment Act (No. 2) 1982) and Tasmania (Justices Act 1959, s.106B as amended by the Justices Amendment Act 1988).

[21] "Personal violence offence" is defined in s.4(1) Crimes Act 1900 and includes every type of personal attack ranging from common assault to murder.

[22] Crimes (Apprehended Violence) Amendment Act 1989, s.562B amending Part XVA Crimes Act 1900 as inserted by the Crimes (Personal and Family Violence) Amendment Act 1987.

[23] As defined below in relation to domestic violence offences.

[24] Crimes Act 1900, s.4(1) as amended by the Crimes (Domestic Violence) Amendment Act 1982, the Crimes (Domestic Violence) Amendment Act 1983, the Crimes (Personal and Family Violence) Amendment Act 1987 and the Crimes (Apprehended Violence) Amendment Act 1989.

[25] For example, the police have wider powers of entry in such cases, (ss.357F–357H of the Crimes Act 1900) and there are special bail procedures which enable the police to impose conditions on the person bailed for the protection of the victim and allow the victim to challenge bail, (Bail Act 1978 as amended by the Bail (Personal and Family Violence) Amendment Act 1987 and the Crimes (Apprehended Violence) Amendment Act 1989).

[26] Crimes (Family Violence) Act 1987, s.3(1).

[27] For a general discussion of the Victorian legislation see R. Ingleby, "The Crimes (Family Violence) Act 1987—a duck or an emu?", (1989) 3 Austr. J. Fam. Law 49.

3.11 In the United States of America every state (except Arkansas and New Mexico) has a statute under which civil protection orders may be obtained for domestic violence. Spouses are eligible to apply for protection under all of these statutes, and former spouses, cohabitants and former cohabitants may also apply in the vast majority of cases. In forty-two states, any family member may apply, regardless of whether they have ever lived in the same household. Household members related by blood or marriage may apply in forty-three states, and unrelated household members and former household members in twenty-four states. Persons with a child in common may apply in thirty states.[28]

3.12 By comparison, the legislation in New Zealand is more restrictive.[29] Under the Domestic Protection Act 1982, non-molestation and non-violence orders are available to men and women who are or have been "living together in the same household".[30] This was fairly narrowly interpreted by the High Court, which has held that the Act applies only to those living together in the same household as spouses, de jure or de facto, and not to relationships involving a parent and child[31] or brother and sister.[32]

3.13 Anyone who falls outside the scope of the domestic violence legislation will be dependent for protection either upon the ordinary law of tort, or, if they are involved in matrimonial or some other family proceedings, upon the inherent jurisdiction of the higher courts to grant injunctions to protect parties to these proceedings.[33] Ostensibly, the higher courts' powers to grant injunctions are very wide: injunctions may be granted "in all cases in which it appears to the court just and convenient to do so".[34] However, in common law actions they will only be granted ancillary to an existing cause of action; there must be a sufficient link between the cause of action and the relief sought by the injunction; and an injunction will generally be granted only in support of a recognised legal or equitable right.[35] It was confirmed by the House of Lords in *Richards* v. *Richards*[36] that these broad principles apply in family cases also.

3.14 But exactly what rights will the law protect? In common law actions, the courts will grant an injunction in respect of actual or threatened tortious behaviour, such as assault and battery, trespass or nuisance. In *Patel* v. *Patel*,[37] an action in trespass, the Court of Appeal upheld an order that the plaintiff's son-in-law should not assault or molest him or trespass on his property but expressly approved the removal of part of an original injunction which had created an exclusion zone of 50 yards around the plaintiff's home. It was held that as a "number of the allegations in the various affidavits that are before us do not constitute a tort, nor give any reason for thinking that a tort might be committed . . . merely to approach within 50 yards of a person's house does not give a cause of action which may be restrained by an injunction in those terms."[38] This illustrates one of the main disadvantages of a tort action compared to the domestic violence legislation. Although an injunction will be granted if a battery or assault,[39] trespass or nuisance can be proved, the behaviour complained of may not amount to this on the facts of the case. The court will not grant an injunction in a common law action in respect of behaviour which does not amount to a

---

[28] P. Finn, "Statutory Authority in the Use and Enforcement of Civil Protection Orders Against Domestic Abuse", (1989) 23 F.L.Q. 43.

[29] W. R. Atkin, D. Sleek and V. Ullrich, "Protecting the victims of domestic violence—the Domestic Protection Act 1982", (1984) 14 V.U.W.L.R. 119.

[30] ss.4, 13, 19 and 20.

[31] *G.* v. *G.* (1987) 4 N.Z.F.L.R. 492.

[32] *Department of Social Welfare* v. *H.* (1987) 4 N.Z.F.L.R. 397. Although in this case, Family Court Judge Inglis expressed the view that the girl concerned needed a non-molestation and non-violence order of the kind only available under the Domestic Protection Act 1982 and that it would have been in the interests of justice for such an order to be made had he the jurisdiction to do so. This is discussed in (1988-9) 27 J. Fam. Law 237.

[33] See para. 2.22 above.

[34] Supreme Court Act 1981, s.37; County Courts Act 1984, s.38.

[35] *Siskina* v. *Distos Compania Naviera S. A.* [1979] A.C. 210, 256, *per* Lord Diplock; *South Carolina Insurance Co.* v. *Assurantie Maatschappij "De Zeven Provincien" N. V.* [1987] A.C. 24, 40, *per* Lord Brandon. Also see S. M. Cretney and J. M. Masson, *Principles of Family Law*, (5th ed.), (1990), pp. 203-205.

[36] [1984] A.C. 174, 218, *per* Lord Brandon.

[37] [1988] 2 F.L.R. 179.

[38] *Per* May L. J. at 180H. See the analysis of this by Judge Fricker, Q.C. in "Molestation and Harassment after *Patel* v. *Patel*", (1988) 18 Fam. Law 395, 400, who argues that it is inappropriate in a common law action to grant an injunction which forbids "molestation" or "harassment" and that such injunctions should only forbid explicit forms of tortious conduct raised in the statement of claim.

[39] *Egan* v. *Egan* [1975] Ch. 218.

tort[40] or a threatened tort, however, greatly it may annoy or distress the person subjected to it.[41]

3.15 Yet behaviour which does not necessarily amount to a tort or a threatened tort can be prohibited under the domestic violence legislation, which can deal with any form of behaviour which has an effect upon the victim sufficiently severe to warrant the intervention of the court. The domestic violence legislation also has a number of other practical advantages. The procedures are comparatively swift and simple and the remedies are directed towards regulating the respondent's behaviour in the future, with the protection of the applicant being the main aim. Thus an injunction can be obtained without delay and without having to undertake to pay damages if it later turns out that it should not have been granted.[42] On the other hand, an important function of actions in tort is to provide compensation for past wrongs and although they can provide protection for the future, this is less frequently their main purpose. Accordingly, they are governed by the normal civil procedures which are slower and less appropriate for cases in which emergency protection may be required. The scope of injunctions in tort actions is also narrower. Hence, it will not ordinarily be possible to obtain an injunction to exclude the defendant from an area around the home, or to prevent him calling at the plaintiff's place of work or the children's school, because of the requirement to prove at least a threatened tort, instead of simply molestation. Finally, there are differences in relation to enforcement. Powers of arrest can only be attached to injunctions made between spouses or a man and woman living with each other in the same household as husband and wife.[43]

3.16 Thus in the context of family proceedings it has come to be recognised that violence and molestation within family relationships need to be treated as a special case. In wardship proceedings, for example, the courts frequently make orders for the protection of children which are very wide-ranging and cover matters such as prohibiting someone from communicating with a ward or seeking to discover the ward's whereabouts. This type of order cannot be justified on the basis of strict legal rights as no such right could conceivably be violated in such circumstances. A more acceptable explanation is that such orders are based on a general jurisdiction to protect the welfare of children deriving from the *parens patriae* jurisdiction of the Crown.[44] Because the need for protection in troubled family relationships has been recognised, the courts have struggled to give protection in other cases where the juristic basis for such protection is not entirely clear.[45] For example, the court's general power in matrimonial cases to protect a party when divorce proceedings are pending[46] has been extended to cover the granting of injunctions after a decree absolute has been made.[47] In *Wilde* v. *Wilde*,[48] the Court of Appeal upheld an ouster order against the former husband (who was still a joint owner of the property) granted in matrimonial proceedings after decree absolute on the basis that there is an inherent jurisdiction to grant an injunction in the interests of the children.[49] It has also been held on several occasions that orders for the protection of children made after decree absolute may include terms for the protection of the former spouse,[50] although as these decisions were reached before *Richards* it is debatable whether they could now be decided on exactly the same basis. There are, however, also instances (including one case decided after *Richards*) in which non-molestation orders have been made after decree absolute to protect a former spouse, without any reference to children.[51]

---

[40] Examples might include following or intercepting someone in the street, making nuisance telephone calls, sending menacing letters and sitting in a car outside someone's house for long periods.

[41] Although it has been suggested that there is a general tort of harassment, see *Thomas* v. *N.U.M.* [1986] Ch. 20 *per* Scott J., the current position is that there is not.

[42] Practice Direction [1974] 1 W.L.R. 576.

[43] Domestic Violence and Matrimonial Proceedings Act 1976, s.2.

[44] A. Bainham, "Household Pests", (1989) 105 L.Q.R. 9, 11.

[45] Cretney and Masson, *op. cit.*, p. 212.

[46] e.g. *Silverstone* v. *Silverstone* [1953] P. 174; *Winstone* v. *Winstone* [1960] P. 28.

[47] In *Montgomery* v. *Montgomery* [1965] P. 46, it was held that after a decree of judicial separation, there being no further proceedings pending, the court had no power to exclude a husband from the matrimonial home in which the wife had no proprietary interest, but an injunction was granted restraining the husband from molesting the wife and from interfering with her occupation of the home.

[48] [1988] 2 F.L.R. 83.

[49] Although there is a conflicting Court of Appeal decision as to whether an inherent jurisdiction to exclude one parent from the house in the interests of the children can be reconciled with *Richards*; *M.* v *M.* [1988] 1 F.L.R. 225. See working paper No. 113, paras. 4.2–4.6.

[50] *Stewart* v. *Stewart* [1973] Fam. 21; *Phillips* v. *Phillips* [1973] 1 W.L.R. 615.

[51] *Ruddell* v. *Ruddell* (1967) 111 S.J. 497; *Webb* v. *Webb* [1986] 1 F.L.R. 541.

3.17 The need to extend the scope of injunctions in family proceedings beyond the scope of the law of tort has been explained by reference to the special nature of family relationships.[52] When problems arise in close family relationships, the strength of emotions involved can cause unique reactions which may at times be irrational or obsessive. Whilst these reactions may most commonly arise between spouses and cohabitants, they can also occur in many other close relationships which give rise to similar stresses and strains and in which the people concerned will often continue to be involved with one another.[53] The object of the law should be to provide a framework to enable people in this situation to continue their relationship in a civilised fashion. Compensation for past transgressions is rarely appropriate (even if it is possible) as when the parties are living in a common household they generally share the same budget. Spouses and cohabitants are given protection in such circumstances and it seems inappropriate, when we are concerned with issues of personal protection from harassment and violence, to require other applicants who are in a very similar situation to point to the infringement of a legal or equitable right before they can obtain a remedy. The policy arguments against requiring an application to be grounded in a legal or proprietary right are particularly strong where there are children in the household. It is inappropriate for the court's ability to step in to protect the welfare of children to depend upon the existence of some technical right in the children themselves or in their adult carer.[54]

3.18 Our proposal in the working paper to maintain the present level of protection and extend it to former spouses, former cohabitants and perhaps parents or people with parental responsibility for the same child[55] met with broad acceptance. No one who responded to the working paper suggested that the protection available at present should be reduced, and many people commented on the need to extend it, particularly to former spouses and former cohabitants. Several practitioners who responded made the specific point that a high proportion of their domestic violence case load consisted of former wives and former cohabitants and said that the failure of the present legislation explicitly to provide protection for these two groups caused a great deal of difficulty in practice. In their experience, bitterness commonly persisted long after separation, especially where one party was unable to accept that the relationship had come to an end. In our view, the case for extending protection to former spouses and former cohabitants is inescapable, and it should be possible for a non-molestation order to be made in favour of a spouse or former spouse or for a man or woman who is living or has lived with the respondent as man and wife. We do not consider the adoption of a "household" test to be necessary in the sense of requiring spouses and cohabitants to be or to have been living in the same household. This would introduce a new requirement in the case of spouses and could reduce the protection available under the present law. In the case of people living together as husband and wife, such a requirement seems unnecessary given that "living with each other as husband and wife" has been held to connote something more than living in the same household,[56] and that cohabitation in the sense of living together as husband and wife can continue although the parties are actually living apart through force of circumstances.[57]

3.19 Many respondents, however, regarded the proposal made in the working paper as too conservative, and urged us to consider extending the range of people protected by this legislation to include other groups. As we see it, there are three possible choices:

(i) to adopt the limited extension suggested in the working paper;

(ii) to remove all restrictions on applicants and throw the jurisdiction open to all as has been done in some Australian states; or

(iii) to choose a middle path and widen the range of applicants to include anyone who is associated with the respondent by virtue of a family relationship or something closely akin to such a relationship.

---

[52] For instance, "This court in its matrimonial jurisdiction has to control situations and problems . . . which are peculiar to it", *Montgomery* v. *Montgomery* [1965] P. 46, *per* Ormrod J. at p. 51D; "This Division of the High Court deals with problems somewhat different from those of other Divisions", *Silverstone* v. *Silverstone* [1953] P. 174, *per* Pearce J. at p. 177; "It may be that the grant of such injunctions can be justified by reference to the distinctive nature of a divorce suit, which does not conclude in quite the same way as other actions", Cretney and Masson, *op. cit.*, p. 212.

[53] For example, *Egan* v. *Egan* [1975] Ch. 218 (mother and son); *Tabone* v. *Seguna* [1986] 1 F.L.R. 591 (mother and daughter's cohabitant); *Patel* v. *Patel* [1988] 2 F.L.R. 179 (father-in-law and son-in-law); *Harrison* v. *Lewis* [1988] 2 F.L.R. 339 (parents of the same child who had never lived together).

[54] Bainham, *op. cit.*, pp. 12–13.

[55] See working paper No. 113, para. 6.56.

[56] *Fuller* v. *Fuller* [1973] 1 W.L.R. 730.

[57] *Santos* v. *Santos* [1972] Fam. 247.

On reflection, we have concluded that the third is the best alternative. The first might exclude people who have a genuine need for protection in circumstances which most people would regard as family relationships in the broader sense. We have in mind instances such as two people who have lived together on a long term basis whether as close friends or in a homosexual relationship. We think that the second alternative goes too far. We do not think it is appropriate that this jurisdiction should be available to resolve issues such as disputes between neighbours, harassment of tenants by landlords or cases of sexual harassment in the workplace. Here there is no domestic or family relationship to justify special remedies or procedures and resort should properly be had to the remedies provided under property or employment law. Family relationships can, however, be appropriately distinguished from other forms of association. In practice, many of the same considerations apply to them as to married or cohabiting couples. Thus the proximity of the parties often gives unique opportunities for molestation and abuse to continue; the heightened emotions of all concerned give rise to a particular need for sensitivity and flexibility in the law; there is frequently a possibility that their relationship will carry on for the foreseeable future; and there is in most cases the likelihood that they will share a common budget, making financial remedies inappropriate.

3.20 Extending applications for non-molestation orders to people associated through a family relationship has the further advantage of being consistent with the recommendations about applications for occupation orders made later in this report.[58] Hence we are able to recommend that entitled applicants (that is, people who have a legal or beneficial interest in or a contractual or statutory right to occupy the property in question) should be able to apply for occupation orders and non-molestation orders against the same classes of people, that is, those with whom they are associated through a family relationship. We could see no good reason for insisting that such applicants should use tortious remedies and denying them access to the wider, more flexible, cheaper and simpler remedies available under the domestic violence legislation. This is of considerable practical importance as occupation orders and non-molestation orders are very often sought at the same time and it could cause confusion if both remedies were not necessarily available between the same parties.

3.21 Having chosen to base our recommendations upon association through family relationship, it becomes necessary to define the relationships in question. We have not found this to be an easy task, but have eventually settled upon six types of relationship in addition to spouses, cohabitants, former spouses and former cohabitants. The first is anyone who lives or has lived in the same household as the respondent, otherwise than merely by reason of one of them being the other's employee, tenant, lodger or boarder. This is intended to include people who live in the same household, other than on a purely commercial basis. It would, for example, exclude a student renting the spare bedroom or a live-in nanny employed to care for children. The phrase "living in the same household" may be expected to retain the usual meaning which it has acquired in matrimonial proceedings.[59] Thus, it is possible for people to live in different households, although they are actually living in the same house. The crucial test is the degree of community life which goes on. If the parties shut themselves up in separate rooms and cease to have anything to do with each other, they live in separate households. But if they share domestic chores and shopping, eat meals together or share the same living room, they are living in the same household, however strained their relations may be.[60]

3.22 We recognise that this approach may on occasions involve distinctions which at first sight seem strange. For example, remedies may be available under this jurisdiction to three or four friends sharing a flat if they are all joint tenants, but not between the one who takes a tenancy and sublets to his friends. Nevertheless, however similar the factual circumstances may appear, the legal relationship of landlord and tenant is quite unlike that of equal household sharers and our recommendations are designed to preserve that distinction. Thus, the category of people living in the same household is needed to cover people such as those mentioned in paragraph 3.19 above, the close friends who have lived together on a long term basis, whatever the precise nature of their relationship.

3.23 The second category includes immediate relatives, whether blood relatives or relatives by affinity, including in the case of cohabitants, people who would have been relatives,

---

[58] See para. 4.9 below.

[59] See further, S. M. Cretney and J. M. Masson, *Principles of Family Law*, (5th ed.), (1991), pp. 124–5.

[60] e.g. *Mouncer* v. *Mouncer* [1972] 1 W.L.R. 321.

had the parties been married. Applications can still be made in respect of these categories of people after divorce or after cohabitation has ceased. We are satisfied that there is a need to cover these cases, which are not always adequately provided for under the present law of tort.[61]

3.24 A further group important in terms of the extent of the problems which can arise, although difficult to define in legislative terms, includes people who have been boyfriend and girlfriend in a romantic relationship which might have varying degrees of sexual involvement. Such relationships are possibly easier to recognise than to describe, but we envisage that there would have been a degree of mutuality and some participation in consensual sexual activity, although not necessarily amounting to sexual intercourse. This group would not include an unbalanced stranger who develops an obsession from a distance, as this would not involve the required family association. However, rejection at even an early stage of a relationship which has begun on a mutual basis can have a devastating effect and give rise to surprisingly odd and obsessive behaviour which quickly becomes frightening or intimidating to the person seeking to end the relationship. We consider that people in this position have just as great a need for, and possibly even more justification for seeking, protection as have spouses and cohabitants whose relationships have broken down. In addition couples who are or have been engaged to marry one another are equally worthy of protection. However, it may be that the couple have neither cohabited nor have a sexual relationship and hence we consider that couples who are engaged or have at any time agreed to marry each other should be covered in a separate category.

3.25 The final categories cover people who are parents of a child or, in relation to any child, are persons who have or have had parental responsibility for that child and people who are parties to the same family proceedings. Although these categories will often overlap, they will not always necessarily do so. These categories are needed to ensure that it is always possible for a non-molestation order, in appropriate circumstances, to be attached to any order made under the Children Act 1989. Such orders were sometimes attached to custody orders under the Guardianship of Minors Acts[62] and may similarly be necessary in proceedings under the 1989 Act. Such a provision, together with power for the court to make orders of its own motion in family proceedings[63] should ensure that all eventualities are covered. Parents may never have lived together,[64] and people with parental responsibility might not fall into any of the other categorties mentioned above. However, in common with these other categories, concern and responsibility for a child's welfare can give rise to strong emotions and unreasonable behaviour. An extreme example of a situation in which such protection would be needed might be a case in which children are fostered or adopted after their father has killed their mother.[65] If the father discovers the children's whereabouts after his release from prison, their new carers might well wish to seek protection against molestation, particularly in view of his history of violence.

3.26 We therefore *recommend* that a non-molestation order should be capable of being made between people who are associated with one another in any of the following ways:

   (i) they are or have been married to each other;

  (ii) they are cohabitants or former cohabitants;

 (iii) they live or have lived in the same household, otherwise than merely by reason of one of them being the other's employee, tenant, lodger or boarder;

 (iv) they are within a defined group of close relatives;[66]

  (v) they have at any time agreed to marry each other (whether or not that agreement has been terminated);

 (vi) they have or have had a sexual relationship with each other (whether or not including sexual intercourse);

---

[61] See, for example, *Patel* v. *Patel* [1988] 2 F.L.R. 179; *Tabone* v. *Seguna* [1986] 1 F.L.R. 591.

[62] *Re W. (a minor)* [1981] 3 All E.R. 401.

[63] See para. 5.3 below.

[64] e.g. *Harrison* v. *Lewis* [1988] 2 F.L.R. 339.

[65] *Re D.* [1991] Fam. 137.

[66] These are defined in clause 27 of the draft Bill as, in relation to a person:

    (a) the father, mother, stepfather, stepmother, son, daughter, stepson, stepdaughter, grandmother, grandfather, grandson or granddaughter of that person or of that person's spouse or former spouse, or

    (b) the brother, sister, uncle, aunt, niece, nephew (whether of the whole blood or of the half blood or by affinity) of that person or of that person's spouse or former spouse,

and includes, in relation to a person who is living or has lived with another person as husband and wife, any person who would fall within paragraphs (a) or (b) if the parties were married to each other.

(vii) they are the parents of a child or, in relation to any child, are persons who have or have had parental responsibility for that child (whether or not at the same time);

(viii) they are parties to the same family proceedings.

(b) *The children concerned*

3.27 The remedies in question are essentially those which an adult may seek, against another adult with whom he or she is associated, either for his or her own sake or for the sake of a child concerned. The working paper suggested that the children protected might include any child of or living with either party.[67] This was, in effect, a combination of the various provisions of the present law.[68] On reflection, however, we do not think it necessary for the court to be required automatically to consider the interests of (or to have power to make orders concerning) every child of either party. It may be quite unnecessary, for example, for the court to consider a child of one party's previous relationship who is now living with the other parent. On the other hand, there might be other children whose interests were indeed relevant in the circumstances of the case. Hence we propose that the court should have power to make orders for the protection of any "relevant child" (and for an occupation order, should be required to consider the interests of any relevant child).[69] This would be defined as any child who is living with or might reasonably be expected to live with either party, any child in relation to whom an order under the Children Act 1989 or the Adoption Act 1976 is in question and any other child whose interests the court considers to be relevant. We do not in general think that there is much real risk of people applying for orders in relation to children for whom they have otherwise no responsibility; but it is clearly desirable for the court to have a discretion to make orders in relation to as wide a range of children as possible, without necessarily being required to consider the position of children whose interests may be completely unaffected by the issues before the court. Hence, the only classes of children automatically included are those whose interests will amost certainly be relevant in every case, because they are living with or might be expected to live with one of the parties or because the question of their welfare is already before the court. It is important that the court hearing proceedings under the Children Act or Adoption Act should have power to protect the child involved in those proceedings against all forms of molestation and abuse. Other children would not be included automatically, but the court could do so in any case where it decided that their interests were relevant. To enlarge on the example above, the court might consider the interests of a child living with the other parent to be relevant if he frequently had long periods of staying access with one of the parties. We hope that this definition, together with provision for non-molestation orders to be made between people who are parties to the same family proceedings and power for the court to make such orders of its own motion or on application in any family proceedings, will ensure that orders can be obtained for the protection of children whenever they are necessary and appropriate.

Duration

3.28 In the working paper[70] we suggested that non-molestation orders should be made for any specified period or until further order. No distinction should be drawn on the basis of the class of applicant as protection should be available when and for as long as it is needed. Fixed time limits are inevitably arbitrary and can restrict the courts' ability to react flexibly to problems arising within the family. In particular, it is important that non-molestation orders should continue to be capable of enduring beyond the end of a relationship, although in some cases, short-term relief will be all that is necessary or desirable. For the reasons given earlier[71] we do not think that a formal distinction between short and long term remedies is necessary in this context. Accordingly, we *recommend* that non-molestation orders should be capable of being made for any specified period or until further order.

---

[67] Paras. 6.11–6.13; 6.59.

[68] The Domestic Violence and Matrimonial Proceedings Act 1976 refers to "a child living with the applicant", the Domestic Proceedings and Magistrates' Courts Act 1978 refers to "a child of the family" and the Matrimonial Homes Act 1983 refers to "any children".

[69] See paras. 4.20–4.34 below.

[70] At para. 6.23.

[71] See para. 2.43 above.

PART IV

OCCUPATION ORDERS

Scope

4.1 A major objective of reform is to remove the present confusion[1] between ouster orders,[2] occupation orders,[3] and exclusion orders.[4] The working paper proposed[5] a rationalisation of the present mixture of orders which are available and this approach commanded substantial support on consultation. We therefore propose that the court should simply have power to make an occupation order, and that this order should be capable of providing for a number of different matters. There is in principle a difference between orders which declare, confer or extend occupation rights ("declaratory orders") and other orders, including ouster orders, which just control the exercise of existing rights ("regulatory orders"). It seems appropriate to treat these categories of order differently because distinctions in the nature of the orders mean that they necessarily require different criteria.

4.2 We therefore *recommend* that the court should have power to make an occupation order with a variety of possible terms, either declaratory or regulatory. The declaratory orders would be those:

   (i) declaring pre-existing occupation rights in the home;

   (ii) extending statutory occupation rights beyond the terminaton of the marriage on divorce or death;

   (iii) granting occupation rights in the home to non-entitled applicants[6] ("an occupation rights order").

The regulatory orders available would be those:

   (iv) requiring one party to leave the home;

   (v) suspending occupation rights and/or prohibiting one party from entering or re-entering the home, or part of the home;

   (vi) requiring one party to allow the other to enter and/or remain in the home;

   (vii) regulating the occupation of the home by either or both of the parties;

   (viii) terminating occupation rights; and

   (ix) excluding one party from a defined area in the vicinity of the home.

4.3 We discuss the criteria appropriate for regulatory orders at paragraphs 4.20–4.34 below. Of the declaratory orders, occupation rights orders (that is, orders granting occupation rights to those who do not already have them) are a separate case requiring special preliminary or qualifying criteria which we disuss at paragraphs 4.10–4.13 below. Orders declaring existing rights of occupation (whether these are statutory rights under what is now the Matrimonial Homes Act 1983 ("matrimonial home rights") or rights of occupation arising from a legal or beneficial interest in the property) do not need criteria as in principle these rights exist automatically and independently of the merits of enforcing or retaining them. The final category is orders which extend matrimonial home rights beyond the termination of the marriage on death or divorce. We *recommend* that these should have their own broad criteria requiring the court to make an order when it considers that this would be just and reasonable in all the circumstances.[7] Under the present law, the court has power to extend statutory rights of occupation beyond the termination of the marriage on death or divorce "in the event of a matrimonial dispute or estrangement". This power is, however, expressed as something of an afterthought and its clarity could be improved.[8]

---

[1] To some of which Judge Fricker Q.C. and the Circuit Judges drew attention; see [1990] Fam. Law 225, at p. 227.

[2] Under the Domestic Violence and Matrimonial Proceedings Act 1976 or the ancillary jurisdiction.

[3] Under the Matrimonial Homes Act 1983.

[4] Under the Domestic Proceedings and Magistrates' Courts Act 1978.

[5] See working paper No. 113, paras. 6.48 and 6.50.

[6] This term is explained at para. 4.5 below.

[7] The criteria designed for regulatory orders are inappropriate, e.g. a criterion relating to the parties' respective housing needs is inapplicable if one party has died.

[8] Matrimonial Homes Act 1983, s.2(4) provides that:

    "Notwithstanding that a spouse's rights of occupation are a charge on an estate or interest in the dwelling house, those rights shall be brought to an end by:

      (a) the death of the other spouse, or

      (b) the termination (otherwise than by death) of the marriage,

    unless in the event of a matromonial dispute or estrangement the court sees fit to direct otherwise by an order made under section 1 above during the subsistence of the marriage."

It is also uncertain exactly what is meant by a "matrimonial dispute or estrangement", although this would presumably cover matrimonial litigation and separation.[9] Giving the court express jurisdiction to make an order extending matrimonial home rights beyond divorce or death would resolve these uncertainties, although if the court were to make an order extending rights of occupation beyond death, it would generally be appropriate for some time limit or condition to be imposed on it.[10]

The home

4.4. At present, under the Matrimonial Homes Act 1983, the court has power to regulate the occupation of an existing or former matrimonial home. There is no power to make orders in respect of a property in which the parties intended to have their home but have not actually lived together. This creates potential problems. For example, a couple might sell their existing home and live in temporary rented accommodation whilst renovating a new one, bought in the man's sole name. If the relationship broke down before the family moved into the new house, the woman would not be entitled to matrimonial home rights in respect of the new property and the court would have no jurisdiction to regulate its occupation, even though it was bought with the intention of being a home for the family and may be the only place available for the mother and children to live. This problem is not confined to married couples, but may extend also to people who have not been married or, indeed have not previously lived together. There has, for example, been a need to regulate occupation rights in a case where a joint council tenancy was granted to a couple with a baby, but whose relationship broke down when only one of them had actually moved in.[11] We therefore *recommend* that the court should have power to make an occupation order in respect of any dwelling-house which is, was or was intended to be the joint home of the parties.

Parties

4.5 Potential applicants for occupation orders fall into two main categories: those who are entitled to occupy the home by virtue of a legal or beneficial estate or interest or a contractual or statutory right, including rights of occupation in the matrimonial home at present granted by the Matrimonial Homes Act 1983 ("entitled applicants"), and those who are not ("non-entitled applicants"). In the case of spouses, (unless they are bare licensees or squatters) both parties will invariably be entitled to occupy the home, either because it is jointly owned or tenanted (as increasing proportions of matrimonial homes now tend to be) or because the non-owning spouse will have matrimonial home rights.[12] In the working paper, we identified a need to extend the court's power to regulate occupation between spouses to entitled cohabitants.[13] This is already the law in Scotland,[14] and the desirability of bringing our own law into line was widely accepted on consultation. These remedies should also be available to a solely entitled applicant in respect of anyone who falls within the relevant categories, although the respondent has no right to occupy the property.

4.6 We consider that entitled applicants should be able to obtain an occupation order against anyone within the same classes of associated people in respect of whom they could obtain a non-molestation order.[15] These applicants have a right to occupy their home which should be enforceable both against people without such a right and people who are jointly entitled to occupy where the circumstances are such that the applicant can satisfy the specified criteria.[16] This is of particular importance in cases of domestic violence as where the parties live together, an occupation order ousting the respondent from the home will often be the only way of supporting a non-molestation order and giving the applicant effective protection.

4.7 We favour drawing a distinction between entitled and non-entitled applicants for two reasons. First, the grant of an occupation order can severely restrict the enjoyment of property rights, and its potential consequences to a respondent are therefore more serious

---

[9] P. M. Bromley and N. V. Lowe, *Bromley's Family Law*, (7th ed.), (1987), p. 548.

[10] For instance, the spouse might be permitted to occupy the dwelling house for a certain length of time or until a certain event occurred, such as the conclusion of a claim under the Inheritance (Provision for Family and Dependants) Act 1975.

[11] *Tuck* v. *Nicholls* [1989] 1 F.L.R. 283.

[12] See para. 2.23 above.

[13] See working paper No. 113, para. 6.4.

[14] Matrimonial Homes (Family Protection) (Scotland) Act 1981, s.18(3).

[15] See para. 3.26 above.

[16] See para. 4.33 below.

than those of a non-molestation order which generally only prohibits conduct which is already illegal or at least, anti-social. Such consequences may be acceptable when both parties are entitled to occupy, but they are more difficult to justify when the applicant has no such right. Also, the purpose of an occupation order is generally different in the two cases. In the case of entitled applicants, particularly where the respondent is also entitled, an occupation order has a purpose beyond short term protection, namely to regulate the occupation of the home until its medium or long term destiny has been decided,[17] or in some cases, indefinitely.[18] Where the respondent is not entitled, an entitled applicant would, of course, have the remedies of an ordinary owner available to her, but an occupation order might well have advantages over these in terms of speed or enforcement, particularly in the context of a violent relationship. There is certainly no reason to place a solely entitled applicant in a worse position than a jointly entitled one for this purpose. In the case of non-entitled applicants, an occupation order is essentially a short term measure of protection intended to give them time to find alternative accommodation, or, at most, to await the outcome of an application for a property law remedy.

4.8 It has been clear since *Davis* v. *Johnson*[19] that ouster orders can be made for the benefit of non-entitled cohabitants, and no-one has suggested to us that this protection should be removed. We proposed in the working paper that protection should be extended to include former spouses and former cohabitants,[20] and this was generally welcomed on consultation, subject to the safeguards mentioned below.[21] We also propose that these remedies would, so far as they are relevant, also be available to a non-entitled applicant in cases where the respondent also has no right to occupy the home.[22] Such cases would probably be comparatively rare, but might arise where the parties are squatters or bare licensees. Orders can at present be obtained by people in this category under the Domestic Violence and Matrimonial Proceedings Act 1976 and the protection at present available would be reduced were we to exclude them from the ambit of our recommendations.

4.9 We accordingly *recommend* that an occupation order should be capable of being made:

(a) in favour of entitled applicants between people who are associated with one another in any of the following ways:

   (i) they are or have been married to each other;

   (ii) they are cohabitants or former cohabitants;

   (iii) they live or have lived in the same household otherwise than merely by reason of one of them being the other's employee, tenant, lodger or boarder;

   (iv) they are within a defined group of close relatives;[23]

   (v) they have at any time agreed to marry each other (whether or not that agreement has been terminated);

   (vi) they have or have had a sexual relationship with each other (whether or not including sexual intercourse); or

   (vii) they are the parents of a child or, in relation to any child, are persons who have or have had parental responsibility for that child (whether or not at the same time); or

   (viii) they are parties to the same family proceedings;

(b) in favour of non-entitled applicants, between people who are cohabitants, former cohabitants or former spouses.

---

[17] In divorce or judicial separation proceedings under the Matrimonial Causes Act 1973, or a claim under the Married Women's Property Act 1882, s.17.

[18] For example, where a married couple separate and there is no need to sell the home.

[19] [1979] A.C. 264.

[20] See working paper No. 113, paras. 6.3, 6.56, 6.57.

[21] See paras. 4.11, 4.12, 4.18 and 4.19.

[22] There would, for example, be no question of declaring or granting occupation rights or terminating or extending matrimonial home rights in such circumstances. But an ouster order, an order requiring the respondent to permit the applicant to enter or remain or an order regulating the parties' occupation of the property might be needed.

[23] These are defined in clause 27 of the draft Bill as, in relation to a person:

   (a) the father, mother, stepfather, stepmother, son, daughter, stepson, stepdaughter, grandmother, grand-father, grandson or granddaughter of that person or of that person's spouse or former spouse, or

   (b) the brother, sister, uncle, aunt, niece, nephew (whether or the whole blood or of the half blood or by affinity) of that person or of that person's spouse or former spouse,

and includes, in relation to a person who is living with or has lived with another person as husband and wife, any person who would fall within paragraphs (a) and (b) if the parties were married to each other.

Non-entitled applicants

(a) Qualifying criteria

4.10 One of the more undesirable features of the present system is that the criteria for and effects of orders in favour of non-entitled applicants have not been defined. This has led to guidelines which are principally relevant to them also being applied to cases where they may not be so appropriate.[24] We have recommended above that non-entitled applicants should be able to apply for orders only against former spouses, cohabitants or former cohabitants.[25] It should, however, be borne in mind that there are two different sorts of non-entitled applicants, those who are seeking an order against an entitled respondent and those who are seeking an order against a respondent who is also non-entitled. In the latter case, the court is only adjusting occupation rights as between the parties themselves, both of whom may well be subject to almost immediate ejection at the behest of a third party. In the discussion which follows, we are concerned principally with the former case, in which an occupation order is sought by a non-entitled applicant against an entitled respondent. There are several advantages in providing qualifying criteria for the grant of an occupation order in these cases. In particular, this would help to clarify the circumstances in which it is appropriate for an order to be made. The justification for allowing non-entitled applicants to use these remedies is their overriding need for short term protection in cases of domestic violence or for short term accommodation for themselves and their children when a relationship breaks down. But, although many of our respondents would not want to see strict property rights given precedence over the family's need for protection and accommodation, there are a number of arguments against putting these applicants on exactly the same footing as entitled applicants. In the first place, these applicants have no entitlement to occupy, arising either out of a proprietary interest or out of their rights as a spouse (although they may have a claim for property adjustment for themselves or for their children). Some of our respondents also thought that distinctions should be drawn between marriage and the mutual commitments this involves, even if in practice the marriage only lasts for a short while; and cohabitation, in which the unmarried couple choose not to make these commitments, although some obligations may arise with the passage of time or the birth of children. By definition non-entitled applicants are not (or at least are no longer) married.

4.11 In the working paper, we suggested limiting the right of former spouses and cohabitants to apply by reference to pending proceedings or to the time since the relationship ended. However, a fixed time limit is bound to be arbitrary and result in unjust distinctions being made between different couples. In the case of cohabitation, any dispute about whether the qualification had been satisfied could be difficult to resolve. A limit which took account of pending applications for property adjustment orders or property law remedies might encourage prolonged or hopeless applications. Nor does this approach cater for ongoing cohabitation.

4.12 We think it would be preferable to adopt a more discretionary approach which would permit the court to make orders which reflect what might be the parties' legitimate expectations according to the circumstances of each particular case. Relevant factors might include matters such as the length of the relationship, whether it was entered into casually or with some degree of mutual commitment, whether there are any children, whether the applicant is claiming a beneficial interest in the property and the length of time since the relationship ended. This is consistent with the approach adopted in Scotland, where a court considering a non-entitled cohabitant's application for occupancy rights is directed to consider all the circumstances of the case, including the time for which the parties have been living together and whether there are any children of the relationship.[26]

4.13 We therefore *recommend* that where a non-entitled applicant applies for an occupation order the court should be required to consider the following qualifying criteria:

(i) where the parties are cohabitants or former cohabitants the nature of their relationship, the length of time during which they have lived together as husband and wife and whether there are children of both parties or for whom both parties have parental responsibility;

---

[24] e.g. Practice Note [1978] 1 W.L.R. 1123, which creates a normal limitation of three months on the duration of ouster orders in favour of both entitled and non-entitled applicants; see para. 4.35 below.

[25] See para. 4.9 above.

[26] Matrimonial Homes (Family Protection) (Scotland) Act 1981, s.18(2).

(ii) where the parties are former cohabitants or former spouses, the length of time that has elapsed since the marriage was dissolved or annulled or since the parties ceased to live together; and

(iii) the existence of any pending proceedings between the parties for financial provision or relating to the legal or beneficial ownership of the dwelling-house.

(b) Effects

4.14 Under section 1(1) of the Matrimonial Homes Act 1983, statutory rights of occupation are granted to any spouse who cannot claim a right of occupation by virtue of any beneficial interest or under any contract or statute, but whose spouse is entitled to occupy the matrimonial home on one or other of these bases. These matrimonial home rights are also available to a spouse who is a beneficial co-owner, with an equitable, but not a legal interest in the house.[27] We propose that these provisions be re-enacted in the draft Bill. These rights bring with them other provisions designed to give the non-entitled spouse a further degree of security by ensuring that occupation by the non-entitled spouse is equated with occupation by the entitled and these would also be retained.[28] Thus, for example, landlords and mortgagees cannot refuse to accept rent or mortgage instalments tendered by the occupier, or treat the property as vacated by the tenant so as to bring to an end a statutory, assured or secure tenancy.[29] The right to register matrimonial home rights would be preserved, as would the court's power to bring these rights to an end, so as to deal with the impasses which can result from registration in order to protect against dispositions to third parties.[30]

4.15 Cohabitants do not have the benefit of automatic occupation rights under the Matrimonial Homes Act 1983. Nor, indeed, do former spouses, unless a court has already ordered that they should continue.[31] Moreover, the nature and effects of the rights of occupation given to a successful applicant for an ouster order under the Domestic Violence and Matrimonial Proceedings Act 1976 are entirely undefined, and non-entitled applicants who have the benefit of such orders can still be left in a very difficult and uncertain position in relation to landlords and mortgagees.

4.16 The position is much clearer in Scotland, where under the Matrimonial Homes (Family Protection) (Scotland) Act 1981, many of the occupancy rights conferred on non-entitled spouses may be granted to non-entitled cohabitants.[32] But, in contrast to spouses, whose occupancy rights arise automatically by virtue of their married status, a cohabiting partner only has occupancy rights if the court, on application, makes an order to this effect.[33] Occupancy rights in favour of cohabitants can be granted for limited periods only.[34] An order granting occupancy rights will be made only where the applicant and her partner are "living with each other as husband and wife", although they need not be doing so at the date of the application provided the separation is recent. An application for occupancy rights can thus be made by a non-entitled cohabitant during an ongoing relationship, whilst the relationship is breaking down, or after it has broken down. Once occupancy rights have been granted, the applicant can apply to the court for an order regulating the rights of

---

[27] Matrimonial home rights were first enacted by the Matrimonial Homes Act 1967 which was passed principally to reverse the decision of the House of Lords in *National Provincial Bank* v. *Ainsworth* [1965] A.C. 1175 so as to enable those rights to become a charge on the property, enforceable against subsequent purchasers. That Act was amended by the Matrimonial Proceedings and Property Act 1970, s.38 which inserted s.1(9) (now s.1(11) of the 1983 Act) to make it clear that the Act applied to a spouse with an equitable interest in the matrimonial home nothwithstanding that this may of itself confer a right of occupation. This was necessary as an equitable interest in unregistered land cannot be protected and could be defeated by a sale or mortgage by the other spouse.

[28] Now in Matrimonial Homes Act 1983, s.1(5) to (8); see clause 4(2) to (7) of the draft Bill.

[29] Technically, a statutory tenancy ends automatically on vacation, whereas with assured and secure tenancies, secure status is lost.

[30] These powers are at present contained in Matrimonial Homes Act 1983, ss.2(1) and 1(2)(a) respectively.

[31] Matrimonial Homes Act 1983, s.2(4) provides that rights of occupation shall be brought to an end by the death of the other spouse or the termination of the marriage unless in the event of a matrimonial dispute or estrangement the court sees fit to direct otherwise by an order made during the subsistence of the marriage. See para. 4.3 above.

[32] See s.18(3). For a discussion of the Scottish Act see D. I. Nichols and M. C. Meston, *The Matrimonial Homes (Family Protection) (Scotland) Act 1981*, (1982). A study of the operation of this Act has been commissioned by the Scottish Home and Health Department from the Law School at the University of Strathclyde, see A. A. Jackson, M. Robertson and P. Robson, *The Operation of the Matrimonial Homes (Family Protection) (Scotland) Act 1981*, (1988).

[33] Matrimonial Homes (Family Protection) (Scotland) Act 1981, s.18(1).

[34] See para. 4.37 below.

occupancy of the home,[35] or for an exclusion order[36] and becomes entitled to, or to apply for a number of subsidiary and consequential rights.[37] Any orders made under these sections terminate automatically when the applicant's occupancy rights terminate.

4.17 There was substantial support on consultation for occupation remedies having the same affect as have a spouse's rights of occupation under section 1 of the Matrimonial Homes Act 1983. Some people suggested introducing provisions similar to those in the Matrimonial Homes (Family Protection) (Scotland) Act 1981. One reason given for this was that such a right of occupation would give the non-entitled cohabitant a chance to apply to court for a property transfer order for the benefit of any child.[38] It would also enable a tenancy to be "kept alive" pending the determination of that application. The same would apply to former spouses who remain in the house pending resolution of an application for property adjustment under the Matrimonial Causes Act 1973.

4.18 We therefore *recommend* that granting an occupation order in favour of a non-entitled applicant should have an effect similar to spouses' automatic rights of occupation under section 1 of the Matrimonial Homes Act 1983 for the duration of the order. We think that this would be best achieved by requiring the court to consider an application in what is effectively two stages, although in most cases where a non-entitled applicant is applying for rights of occupation and an order regulating or extending such rights the process would in practice be telescoped. Thus, the court would first consider whether in a particular case occupation rights should be granted,[39] and would, in doing so, take into account the three factors set out in paragraph 4.33 below[40] and the qualifying criteria relating to non-entitled applicants set out in paragraph 4.13 above. Having decided in favour of the applicant, the court would then decide whether, on the merits, a regulatory order ought to be made. This would involve reconsidering the three factors from paragraph 4.33 and also taking into account the duty to make an order if the balance of harm test set out in that paragraph is satisfied. We consider that this procedure is desirable to ensure that the qualifying criteria for the grant of occupation rights to non-entitled applicants do not obscure the merits of the applicant's case for the grant of a regulatory order in a situation of overwhelming need. There may, for example, be cases in which the applicant's case for an occupation rights order is not particularly strong (perhaps because she has lived with the respondent only for a matter of weeks) but in which her need is so great that it would nevertheless be just for her application to be granted (perhaps because she is ill, has the respondent's baby to care for and nowhere else to go). We therefore *recommend* accordingly.

4.19 The great majority of respondents tended to see occupation remedies for non-entitled applicants as a relatively short term measure of protection, just to give sufficient time to find alternative accommodation or to await the outcome of property proceedings. We did not suggest in the working paper that occupation rights granted to a non-entitled applicant should be capable of registration as a charge on the property itself as are spouses' rights by virtue of section 2(1) of the Matrimonial Homes Act 1983. Registration of rights which will have a time limit set by the court seems inappropriate. It has to be recognized that such a right would in consequence be merely personal and the owner could sell or mortgage over the head of the occupying applicant, unless the court were willing to grant an injunction to prevent this while the order was in force. Given the relatively short duration of such orders, however, in practice this is unlikely to be much of a problem. We accordingly *recommend* that occupation rights granted to non-entitled applicants should be personal rights only and should not therefore be capable of registration as a charge against the property or be valid against a purchaser.

---

[35] Matrimonial Homes (Family Protection) (Scotland) Act 1981, s.3.

[36] *Ibid.*, s.4.

[37] *Ibid.*, s.2. This section confers various supplementary rights intended to make the right of occupancy effective, for example, authorising the carrying out of obligations of or the enforcing of duties towards the other spouse without his consent, similar to the Matrimonial Homes Act 1983, s.1(5)–(8). It also gives the court power to make orders in relation to the use of furniture and plenishings and to apportion past and future expenditure on the home.

[38] Under the Children Act 1989, Sched. 1, para. 1 (formerly Guardianship of Minors Act 1971, as amended by the Family Law Reform Act 1987).

[39] See para. 4.2 above. These would carry with them consequential rights equivalent to those contained in the Matrimonial Homes Act 1983, s.1(5)–(8).

[40] i.e. (i) the respective housing needs and resources of the parties and of any child who is a child of or is living with either party;
(ii) the respective financial resources of the parties; and
(iii) the likely effect of any order, or of any decision by the court not to make an order, on the health, safety and well-being of the parties and of any such child.

Criteria for regulatory orders

4.20 The criteria for regulatory orders have to reflect the many variations between the different cases to which they will apply:

   (i) the relief sought may vary, for example from the restoration to the home of a person who has been locked out by the other partner, or the regulation of how the various rooms in a large house are to be used pending the determination of divorce and property adjustment proceedings, or the keeping away of a person who has already established an alternative home elsewhere but returns periodically to pester the remaining inhabitants, to the exclusion of a person from premises he regards as his permanent home;

  (ii) the reason for seeking relief may vary, for example from a need for immediate protection against serious violence or abuse, or for an effective remedy in a less serious case in which non-molestation orders have proved useless, or to resolve a dispute about living arrangements during a marital breakdown in which there is no molestation but relations have become intolerably strained, or to confirm the long-term entitlement of a separated spouse to remain in the matrimonial home whether or not a divorce is eventually obtained;

 (iii) the circumstances and perceptions of the parties themselves may vary endlessly, for example from a comfortably-off middle-aged married couple with a home to which they are both deeply attached, to a recently cohabiting "dual income, no kids" couple each of whom can readily arrange alternative accommodation, to a stereotypical family of a mother with two young children and no paid employment and a breadwinner father with a relatively secure income and prospects, to a young unmarried mother living in her own council flat with a new boyfriend who was previously living with his own parents and has no particular attachment to the premises in question.

4.21 Hence the remedy itself may be of extreme seriousness, for example where the application is for the immediate exclusion of a person who has no alternative accommodation available from a home in which he is firmly established. The courts have frequently emphasised that such a grave step is not to be taken lightly or without proper regard for the due processes of the law.[41] Of course, however serious the remedy, it may nevertheless be proper to grant it in the particular circumstances of the case. In other cases, the remedy sought, or the circumstances in which it is sought, may not be of the same degree of gravity. The criteria to be applied by the courts have to be sufficiently flexible to cater appropriately for the very broad range of cases which may arise.

(a) The present criteria—Matrimonial Homes Act 1983

4.22 Under the present law, the criteria for the grant of an ouster or occupation order are those prescribed under the Matrimonial Homes Act 1983,[42] which provides for the court to make such order as it thinks "just and reasonable having regard to the conduct of the spouses in relation to each other and otherwise, their respective needs and financial resources, to the needs of any children and to all the circumstances of the case". None of these factors is expressed to be paramount over any other. However, since the decision in *Richards*, there has been a general trend towards requiring proof of matrimonial misbehaviour on the part of the respondent worse than that on the part of the applicant before granting an ouster order.[43]

4.23 In the working paper, we drew attention to a number of shortcomings in these criteria,[44] and there was almost universal agreement on consultation that they are unsatisfactory. They do not give priority to the applicant's personal protection, but require this to be balanced against all other factors, including hardship to the respondent. Thus the level of protection provided for an applicant suffering from violence may not be adequate. Also, a requirement to decide upon occupation of the family home on the basis (at least in part) of fault, thus encouraging parties to make allegations about behaviour, sits uneasily with the general trend in matrimonial law towards reducing the need for recrimination and fault-finding, and enabling the courts to deal with problems of family breakdown without

---

[41] e.g. *per* Balcombe L.J. in *Whitlock* v. *Whitlock* [1989] 1 F.L.R. 208, 210.

[42] s.1(3), applied to all ouster orders and orders regulating occupation by the House of Lords in *Richards* v. *Richards* [1984] A.C. 174.

[43] See working paper No. 113, paras. 3.9–3.11; *Wiseman* v. *Simpson* [1988] 1 W.L.R. 35, 42 *per* Ralph Gibson L.J.; *Summers* v. *Summers* [1986] 1 F.L.R. 343. Also, M. E. Doggett, "*Scott* v. *Scott*, The Independent, May 13, 1991" [1991] J.S.W.F.L. 397.

[44] See working paper No. 113, paras. 3.1–3.37. The criticisms are summarised in para. 2.26 above.

allocating blame, with a view to enhancing the possibility of agreement or even reconciliation between the parties. The test is also thought to give insufficient weight to the interests of children as the balancing exercise throws the children into the scales along with all the other factors and gives no priority to their welfare. This again is inconsistent with the general trend of the law to give increased, if not predominating weight to the interests of children, even in relation to matters of finance and property.[45] Only two respondents suggested that the Matrimonial Homes Act criteria should remain.[46] This was not on account of any intrinsic merit, but because it was feared that the "balance of hardship test" proposed in the working paper leaned too far in the favour of applicants and could lead to occupation orders almost on demand.

4.24 Thus respondents with a wide variety of perspectives on the problem were united in condemning the present law. There was widespread agreement that changes are needed. The question arises as to what the new criteria should be. Two main candidates emerged, the "balance of hardship test" proposed in the working paper and a test which makes the interests of the children paramount. In considering these, it should be borne in mind that we are generally assuming that both parties will be entitled to occupy the property. Qualifying criteria which may be appropriate in the case of non-entitled applicants have already been discussed above.[47]

(b) Balance of hardship

4.25 In the working paper, we suggested a return to the "balance of hardship" test employed in *Bassett* v. *Bassett*,[48] as described by Cumming-Bruce J.

> "I extract from the cases the principle that the court will consider with care the accommodation available to both spouses, and the hardship to which each will be exposed if an order is granted or refused, and then consider whether it is really sensible to expect [the applicant] and child to endure the pressures which the continued presence of the other spouse will place on them. Obviously inconvenience is not enough. Equally obviously, the court must be alive to the risk that a spouse may be using the instrument of an injunction as a tactical weapon in the matrimonial conflict. . . . Where there are children, whom [the applicant] is looking after, a major consideration must be to relieve them of the psychological stresses and strains imposed by the friction between their parents, as the long term effect upon a child is liable to be of the utmost gravity."

4.26 We accordingly proposed the following criteria. The court should make such order as in all the circumstances is fair, just and reasonable in the light of:

(i) whether the parties can reasonably be expected to live or continue to live under the same roof;

(ii) the parties' respective needs and resources, in particular the hardship caused to each party if the order is made or not made; and

(iii) the welfare of any child concerned, which should be considered both in its own right and in relation to factors (i) and (ii) above.

The "reasonableness" factor in (i) would enable the court to deny the remedy to an obviously undeserving applicant, who had no real reason for wanting to live apart or who was seeking to improve her position in eventual property adjustment proceedings, whilst taking into account the problems of those who need personal protection and the disadvantages of requiring extensive trials of the parties' conduct pending divorce. The balancing of needs and resources and of hardship in (ii) recognises that an ouster order will frequently have a severe effect, but obliges the court to consider how great, in the particular case, the hardship will actually be. It also obliges the court to compare the hardship likely to be caused by making the order with the hardship likely to be caused by refusing it. In either case, the hardship caused to any children, both by making or refusing an order can also be considered. We felt that the formulation of the child's welfare in (iii) would help to indicate to the court its relevance to each of the other factors and give a clearer indication of its relative weight

---

[45] The Matrimonial and Family Proceedings Act 1984 requires courts, when dealing with financial provision and property adjustment after divorce, to give "first consideration" to the welfare of any children of the family who are under 18. See also Matrimonial Causes Act 1973, s.25(1) and Domestic Proceedings and Magistrates' Courts Act 1978, s.3(1).

[46] Family Law Bar Association and the Society of Conservative Lawyers.

[47] Paras. 4.10 to 4.13.

[48] [1975] Fam. 76, 87; see working paper No. 113, paras. 6.27–6.33, 6.62.

than would referring to it as the "first consideration".[49] We hoped to steer a middle course between making the welfare of the children paramount and the present law under which, as a result of the decision in *Richards*, the interests of the adult in remaining in the home must prevail unless his behaviour has been sufficiently bad to justify the consequences to him of ouster. Thus, the child's welfare would not be paramount in the sense that it would prevail no matter how unreasonable it was to expect the parties to stay in the same house or how great the hardship involved, but if brought into account at each stage of the process, it should achieve greater importance than it has at present under the Matrimonial Homes Act 1983.

4.27 Many respondents supported this proposal. The Law Society saw the test as an improvement on the present position in that it obliges the court to consider the hardship caused to the respondent by making the order and compare it with the hardship caused by refusing an order, and also enables any hardship caused to children to be taken into account. Other respondents agreed that the balance of hardship test was the best way to take account of the parties' respective needs and resources. It was also considered to be an appropriate test because it has the advantage of directing the court to concentrate on the needs of the parties and their children, rather than upon fault or conduct, while at the same time permitting greater emphasis to be given to the interests of the children.

4.28 However, some respondents submitted that the immediate safety, health and well-being of the applicant should take precedence over all other considerations. They argued that, in consequence, the criteria for occupation orders should differ according to whether or not the applicant has been a victim of violence or threatened violence. The balance of hardship test was criticised for failing to give sufficient emphasis to this. Details of the proposals varied, but the idea was essentially that there would either be a strong presumption in favour of an ouster order, or that an ouster order would be granted virtually automatically in cases of violence. In other cases, the decision would depend either on the interests of the children or on something similar to the balance of hardship test. Although this model has the advantages of giving the best possible protection to victims and avoiding trials of conduct, it nevertheless has the overwhelming drawback discussed above,[50] in that it provides applicants with a strong incentive to provoke or allege violence to make sure they obtain an order.

(c) Children's welfare paramount

4.29 Our scheme was, however, thought by some other respondents to give insufficient weight to the welfare of the children. Applications for occupation orders under the domestic violence legislation or for ouster orders in matrimonial proceedings are invariably made at a critical time in the lives of children, when the relationship between their parents has broken down, possibly irretrievably, and their family life and security is threatened. It is the general policy of the law to emphasise the responsibilities of parents towards their children and to put the children's interests first in making decisions relating to the family. Arguably, if there is a time when the children's welfare should be paramount, this is it.[51] There is also an argument that if the parents knew that the children's interests would be paramount in any decision about the occupation of the home, it might encourage a more pragmatic and resolute attempt at solving problems of accommodation without self-interested resort to litigation.

4.30 Some respondents accordingly thought that there should be consistency with the Children Act 1989 and that the welfare of the children should be paramount.[52] They argued that a distinction should not be made between decisions relating to the children's upbringing and other decisions such as those involved in domestic violence and occupation of the family home. This could have the undesirable consequence of the court being required to apply two different sets of criteria if it had to make orders under the Children Act 1989 in the context of these proceedings or had to deal with an application for an occupation order in other family proceedings. Two respondents made the point that there are many cases in which, in deciding issues relating to the occupation of the family home, the court is, directly

---

[49] There is some difficulty about whether it is practicable to try to require the courts to give greater priority to the interests of the children without making their interests paramount. Thus it has been argued that it is useless to make a factor the court's "first" consideration as this gives no indication of its relative weight. F. Bennion, "First Consideration: A Cautionary Tale", (1976) 126 N.L.J. 1237.

[50] See paras. 2.44–2.46.

[51] See dicta of Lord Scarman in *Richards* v. *Richards*, [1984] A.C. 174, 212.

[52] Children Act 1989, s.1(1).

or indirectly, also making decisions relating to the care and control of the children and that it is in practice often impossible to distinguish between the two. It was also suggested that if a new statute were to be based on a principle which did not give paramountcy to the interests of the children, there was a risk that subsequent case law might continue to diminish the weight given to the children's interests.

4.31 Other respondents specifically agreed with the suggestion in the working paper[53] that a middle course should be taken which placed the children's interests first but not necessarily paramount over all others. In complete contrast to one of the views expressed above, some people thought that it was irrelevant that "first" consideration gave little indication of its relative weight. They considered that the experience of the courts in interpreting section 25 of the Matrimonial Causes Act 1973 showed that they would have little difficulty in interpreting what was meant. It was also argued that "paramount" gave too much weight to the children's interests, and could lead the court to overlook the vulnerability of women and other dependants. The respondents who took this view thought that, in the context of domestic violence legislation, the violence or abuse was the main issue rather than the interests of the children. The paramountcy test was seen as giving too little weight to the applicant's need for personal protection: in other words, some courts might refuse an order, even if there had been violence, on the ground that it would be better for the children if their parents (or even parent and partner) stayed together. This is contrary to the usual assumption (and that made in *Richards*) that paramountcy will favour the parent with whom the children are to live, usually the mother, who is also usually the applicant for an ouster order. The latter view was taken by the Family Law Bar Association. Although they did not specifically support the proposal in the working paper as they favoured retention of the Matrimonial Homes Act criteria, they objected to making the interests of the child paramount because they considered that this might lead to more specious applications by fathers for custody, and encourage more mothers to use "I've got the kids so kick him out" arguments.

(d) A balance of harm test

4.32 We have not found this debate between the balance of hardship and paramountcy tests an easy one to resolve. Nor do the arguments based on consistency all point the same way. The court faced with deciding issues of the children's residence and the occupation of the family home might find it simpler to treat the children's welfare as paramount throughout. But the court deciding issues of financial provision and property adjustment, whether for them or for the adult parties, must treat their welfare as the first but not paramount consideration.[54] On balance, we have been impressed by the support given to the working paper's approach by a number of legal organisations with extensive experience in family law, but who are neutral in that they do not represent any particular interest group.[55] The balance of hardship test does not appear to have any positive disadvantages. Indeed, most of the respondents who argued in favour of the paramountcy test favoured a balance of hardship test in cases where there were no children. However, as a result of considering the various comments and suggestions made by respondents, we think that the balance of hardship test could be improved.

4.33 We *recommend* that the court should have power to grant a regulatory occupation order in any case after considering all the circumstances of the case and in particular the following factors:

(i) the respective housing needs and resources of the parties and of any relevant child;

(ii) the respective financial resources of the parties; and

(iii) the likely effect of any order, or of any decision by the court not to make an order, on the health, safety and well-being of the parties and of any relevant child.

However, the court should have a duty to make an order if it appears likely that the applicant or any relevant child will suffer significant harm if an order is not made and that such harm will be greater than the harm which the respondent or any relevant child will suffer if the order is made.

4.34 We believe that this approach will enable the courts to cater properly and fairly for the wide range of cases in which occupation orders may be sought. The benefit of such a

---

[53] See working paper No. 113, paras. 6.31–6.32; but see also paras. 6.62–6.63.

[54] e.g. under the Matrimonial Causes Act 1973, s.25(1).

[55] Such as the Magistrates' Association, Solicitors' Family Law Association, Association of Women Solicitors and the Law Society.

test is that it encompasses some of the advantages of each of the alternative approaches suggested by our respondents whilst retaining the basic principles of the test proposed in the working paper. In cases where the question of significant harm does not arise, the court would have power to make an order taking into account the three factors set out above; but, in cases where there is a likelihood of significant harm, this power becomes a duty and the court must make an order after balancing the degree of harm likely to be suffered by both parties and any children concerned. This approach would still work in the case of cross applications, where the court would firstly consider who would suffer the greatest risk of harm if the order were not made. In the event of the balance of harm being equal, the court would retain power to make an order, but would have no duty to do so, and so would still be able to reach the right result. Harm has a narrower meaning than hardship. It is defined as "ill-treatment or impairment of physical or mental health".[56] In relation to children, the term will attract the definition used in section 31 of the Children Act 1989.[57]It is likely that a respondent threatened with ouster on account of his violence would be able to establish a degree of hardship (perhaps in terms of difficulty in finding or unsuitability of alternative accommodation or problems in getting to work). But he is unlikely to suffer significant harm, whereas his wife and children who are being subjected to his violence or abuse may very easily suffer harm if he remains in the house. In this way the court will be treating violence or other forms of abuse as deserving immediate relief, and will be directed to make an order where a risk of significant harm exists. However, by placing an emphasis on the need for a remedy rather than on the conduct which gave rise to that need, the criteria will not actually put a premium on allegations of violence and thus may avoid the problems which would be generated by a scheme which focuses upon it. The proposed test also has the advantage that it will avoid giving rise to a situation in which the court is put in the undesirable position of having to choose between the interests of a child and those of an adult, as, in cases where there is a risk of significant harm to a child, the duty to make an order will come into operation and the child's welfare will effectively become the paramount consideration.

Duration

4.35 Although there is nothing in the Matrimonial Homes Act 1983 to suggest that occupation orders should be temporary, it was emphasised in *Davis* v. *Johnson*[58] that an ouster injunction under the Domestic Violence and Matrimonial Proceedings Act 1976 was essentially a short-term remedy. There is also a Practice Note[59] in force which states that ouster injunctions should normally be limited to three months in the first instance, although its scope is not entirely clear.[60] We suggested in the working paper that these guidelines might be revised, and also that consideration might be given to imposing a statutory time limit for occupation orders granted to non-entitled applicants.[61] A large majority of respondents were in favour of revising the guidelines and confirmed that in their present form they are too inflexible and do not allow sufficient time for proceedings under the Matrimonial Causes Act 1973 or applications for property law remedies to be concluded.[62]

4.36 Time limits are not obviously appropriate to the regulation of occupation between those who have equal rights to occupy, especially spouses who have obligations to provide for one another and may decide to live apart indefinitely while remaining married. In the circumstances, we *recommend* that all occupation orders between spouses whether co-owners or not, and co-owners whether cohabitants or not, should be capable of being made for any specified period or until further order.

---

[56] See clause 27 of the draft Bill.

[57] See Children Act 1989, ss.31(9), (10) and 105(1). "Harm" is defined to include ill-treatment or the impairment of health or development.

[58] [1979] A.C. 264.

[59] [1978] 1 W.L.R. 1123.

[60] Although the Practice Note appears to cover all types of ouster injunction, whether under the 1976 Act or in matrimonial proceedings, it is not clear whether the courts are also to follow these general guidelines in ordinary proceedings under the Matrimonial Homes Act 1983. The Practice Note does not, in any event, fetter the judge's discretion as in appropriate cases, the court has granted an ouster injunction "until further order"; see *Spencer* v. *Camacho* (1983) 4 F.L.R. 662 and *Galan* v. *Galan* [1985] F.L.R. 905.

[61] See working paper No. 113, paras. 6.23-6.24.

[62] The guidelines were produced shortly after the Domestic Violence and Matrimonial Proceedings Act 1976 and the decision in *Davis* v. *Johnson* [1979] A.C. 264 which extended the power to make ouster orders in favour of non-entitled cohabitants. Were a statutory time limit for occupation orders granted to non-entitled cohabitants to be imposed then the Practice Direction would become largely redundant.

4.37 In the case of non-entitled applicants, we suggested[63] that any occupation order might be limited in duration along the Scottish model, which is now a maximum of six months in the first instance with renewal thereafter for periods of up to six months at a time with no overall limit.[64] Initially, occupation orders under the Scottish Act were limited to a maximum of three months in the first instance, but it was found in practice that problems were created and that many applications for extensions were needed because three months was too short a period to enable applicants to examine the options available in regard to their housing needs. Respondents were divided upon whether there should be a statutory time limit, most being in favour of but some against it. In principle, we think that a time limit is desirable. Two reasons were given for opposing one: first, the object sought by granting an order would not be achieved because the applicant would not have sufficient time to find alternative accommodation, and secondly, this might give the respondent the impression that he could recommence his behaviour once the time limit had passed. We think that the latter is likely to arise only in isolated cases and that any such misapprehension can easily be corrected. However we were persuaded, particularly in view of the experience in Scotland, that there is a widespread problem of applicants being unable to find alternative accommodation in less than six months. We therefore *recommend* that occupation orders in favour of non-entitled applicants be limited, as they are in Scotland, to up to six months in the first instance, with the possibility of renewal for up to six months at a time.

Ancillary orders

4.38 The working paper suggested that the court should have power (currently only available in proceedings under the Matrimonial Homes Act 1983) to make ancillary orders as to the discharge of rent, mortgage instalments and other outgoings.[65] This should not delay the principal relief in emergency cases but might be particularly useful when an occupation order continues for some time, perhaps awaiting the outcome of proceedings under the Matrimonial Causes Act 1973 or under the ordinary law of property. This proposal received overwhelming support on consultation. Practitioners commented that at times of crisis, financial matters are often a cause of great concern to clients and it was felt that such a power would be a useful means of clarifying the situation.

4.39 We also suggested that the court might have power to order the occupying party to make payments to the other for that occupation.[66] At present only a non-entitled spouse can be ordered to make such payments but in principle there is no reason why any person who is occupying property which another person is prima facie entitled to occupy, whether solely or jointly, should not in an appropriate case be ordered to compensate the other person. This proposal does not seem to have attracted separate comment from respondents but (in combination with the previous recommendation) might give the court greater scope to achieve a fair result when making occupation orders in favour of some applicants.

4.40 We also sought views upon whether the court should have power to make orders about the use of furniture.[67] These were also intended to be ancillary to an occupation order and to attract the same power to make ancillary financial orders as does the occupation order itself. It is not expected that these would be frequently used, but they do occasionally arise in matrimonial cases at present. This proposal also met with general support.

4.41 As under the present legislation, these are discretionary powers which should only be exercised where they are just and reasonable. They are not intended as a disguised form of maintenance for those who are not entitled to it, although they could be used in part discharge of a maintenance obligation (whether to an adult party or child) which does exist. In an appropriate case, the occupying party might be ordered to discharge outgoings or compensate the other. In other circumstances, the non-occupier may be ordered to discharge outgoings. We also think it would be helpful and would promote consistency to provide statutory criteria to guide the court in deciding whether an order is "just and reasonable".

4.42 We therefore *recommend* that the court should have power to make the following ancillary orders where it just and reasonable to do so:

---

[63] See working paper No. 113, para. 6.24.
[64] Matrimonial Homes (Family Protection) (Scotland) Act 1981, s.18(1), as amended by Law Reform (Miscellaneous Provisions) (Scotland) Act 1985, s.13(9)(a).
[65] See working paper No. 113, paras. 6.18, 6.49(c).
[66] *Ibid.*, para. 6.49(d).
[67] *Ibid.*, paras. 6.20, 6.49(a).

(i) to impose on either party obligations regarding the discharge of rent, mortage instalments and other outgoings;

(ii) to impose on either party obligations as to the repair and maintenance of the home;

(iii) to order payments by the occupying party to an entitled non-occupier for that occupation;

(iv) to grant one party possession or use of furniture or other belongings.

In deciding whether an order under one of the above is just and reasonable, the court should take into account the parties' financial resources and any financial obligations which they have or are likely to have in the foreseeable future, including any financial obligations to each other or to any relevant child. This might include any pending applications, existing maintenance orders or orders under the Child Support Act 1991 and also cases where such applications have been made but have proved unsuccessful.

PART V

COMMON MATTERS

Jurisdiction

5.1 We suggested in the working paper[1] that orders under this jurisdiction might be made on application (by any person entitled to do so) without any other proceedings being instituted, or on application in the course of any family proceedings.[2] This is in line with our objectives of rationalising, simplifying and unifying family law and jurisdiction generally and would, for example, enable a court hearing a dispute about where a child is to live to make a non-molestation order, if this is in the child's interests, and to settle the occupation of the family home as well. Few respondents commented directly on this proposal, but a number of responses favoured removing the present fragmentaion which means that it is not always possible to deal with all the questions likely to arise as a consequence of the same family breakdown at the same time.

(a) Own motion powers

5.2. A more difficult question is whether the court should have power (as it has for most private law orders relating to children) to make orders of its own motion. Our preliminary view[3] was that this might be less appropriate for orders regulating the lives of adults, where it might reasonably be expected that they can decide for themselves when an application is necessary. In relation to children, however, it might be desirable in the interests of those children for the court to react immediately to a situation which has arisen and make an appropriate order. It is also possible to draw a distinction between non-molestation and occupation orders. The former are often truly ancillary to some other remedy and the need for them may only become apparent in the course of the proceedings. They do not prejudice the respondent's interests to any significant extent. Also, an own motion power might be useful on occasions where the victim is being subjected to threats or intimidation or is for some other reason reluctant to make an application for a non-molestation order herself. But whilst an occupation order may be a consequence of some other decision, it is difficult to think of circumstances in which it would be justifiable to make one without an application having been made.

5.3 We therefore *recommend*

  (i) that non-molestation orders should be capable of being made

    (a) on application without any other proceedings having been issued; and

    (b) of the court's own motion or on application in any family proceedings;

  (ii) that occupation orders should be capable of being made on application (by any person entitled) without any other proceedings being instituted or on application in any family proceedings.

(b) Powers of magistrates' courts

5.4 In the working paper we asked whether the magistrates' jurisdiction should be more limited than that of the higher courts. We canvassed several possible limitations. These included excluding cohabitants, excluding molestation and excluding issues relating to property rights.[4] Magistrates can already grant exclusion orders between spouses and most people who responded to the working paper were in favour of giving them a general jurisdiction over cohabitants, occupation (as opposed to property rights) and molestation. To do so would promote the general objective of developing a unified family jurisdiction. There was, however, general agreement that whilst magistrates could deal with short and medium term occupation orders (and could frequently ignore property issues in order to enable themselves to do so) it would be inappropriate for that court to deal with complex disputes relating to ownership or the transfer of tenancies.[5] We therefore *recommend* that all courts should have the same jurisdiction to make non-molestation and occupation orders, but that magistrates' courts should be required to transfer a case or to refuse jurisdiction if a dispute arises as to whether either party has a pre-existing legal, beneficial or statutory

---

[1] Working paper No. 113, para. 6.54.
[2] "Family proceedings" would be defined in the same way as they are defined in s.8(3) and (4) of the Children Act 1989.
[3] See working paper No. 113, para. 6.55.
[4] See working paper No. 113, Appendix B; paras. 6.34 and 6.35.
[5] See paras. 6.1–6.12 below.

right to occupy the home unless it is unnecessary for this to be decided before dealing with the matter. We further *recommend* that, as at present, jurisdiction to order the transfer of tenancies under what is now section 7 of and Schedule 1 to the Matrimonial Homes Act 1983 should be restricted to the higher courts.

Emergencies—ex parte orders

5.5 In the working paper we suggested that the court should have power to make ex parte orders where there is imminent danger of actual bodily harm to the applicant or a child if the order is not made, or where there is reason to believe that the respondent is evading service. The possibility was raised of distinguishing between ex parte non-molestation orders and ex parte occupation orders. This might be done on the basis that whilst the former only restrains the respondent from breaking the law or from other anti-social behaviour, the latter requires a balancing exercise which is difficult to carry out without the benefit of an inter partes hearing. But, although there was some support for this on consultation, the preferred view seemed to be that this would be arbitrary and (as such orders are often applied for together) would restrict the court's ability to grant the necessary protection in an appropriate case. In practice, ex parte occupation orders, particularly ouster orders, are extremely rare.

5.6. It is important to bear in mind that there are a number of inherent drawbacks to ex parte orders. The danger of a misconceived or malicious application being granted or the risk of some other injustice being done to the respondent is inevitably greater where the court has only heard the applicant's side of the story and the respondent has had no opportunity to reply. Also, on ex parte applications, the judge has no opportunity to try to resolve the parties' differences by agreed undertakings or otherwise to reduce the tension of the dispute. Equally, there is no opportunity to bring home the seriousness of the situation to the respondent and to underline the importance of complying with the order or undertaking. These disadvantages have led the courts to emphasise the exceptional nature of ex parte orders and the preferability of abridging time and requiring the respondent to attend on short notice whenever practicable.[6] Nevertheless, despite the accepted need for caution, it is well recognised that there are occasions when ex parte orders are both necessary and desirable. Attention was repeatedly drawn on consultation to the need for ex parte orders in cases of imminent physical violence and it is difficult to think of a more compelling justification, in a proper case, for permitting concern about the inherent dangers of ex parte orders to be outweighed. As Ormrod L. J. has said, ". . . the power of the court to intervene immediately and without notice in proper cases is essential to the administration of justice. But this power must be used with great caution and only in circumstances in which it is really necessary to act immediately. Such circumstances do undoubtedly tend to occur more frequently in family disputes than in other types of litigation because the parties are often still in close contact with one another and, particularly when a marriage is breaking up, in a state of high emotional tension; but even in such cases the court should only act ex parte in an emergency when the interests of justice or the protection of the applicant or a child clearly demands. immediate intervention by the court. Such cases should be extremely rare . . . Circumstances, of course, may arise where prior notice cannot be given to the other side; for example, cases where one parent has disappeared with the children, or a spouse, usually the wife, is so frightened of the other spouse that some protection must be given against a violent response to service of proceedings, but the court must be fully satisfied that such protection is necessary."[7] There are thus two rather different situations in which urgency may be necessary. There are cases in which the remedy is needed urgently in itself, and other cases in which the applicant needs protection from the respondent in order to pursue her remedy in peace, although she may not need the remedy itself with the same degree of urgency.

5.7. At present there are many distinctions between the different courts in relation both to the law and to the procedure governing ex parte applications. Emergency applications can be made ex parte in the High Court and the county courts,[8] but the circumstances in which orders will be granted are restricted.[9] Magistrates' courts have power to make

---

[6] e.g. *G.* v. *G.* [1990] 1 F.L.R. 395; *Wookey* v. *Wookey* [1991] Fam. 121, 131 *per* Butler-Sloss L. J.

[7] *Ansah* v. *Ansah* [1977] Fam. 138, 142, 143, quoted with approval by Lord Donaldson M. R. in *G.* v. *G.* [1990] 1 F.L.R. 395, 398.

[8] R.S.C., O.29, r.1; C.C.R., O.13, r.6(3).

[9] Practice Note (Matrimonial Causes: Injunctions) [1978] 1 W.L.R. 925. This is, in fact, phrased in more restrictive terms than the account given by Ormrod L. J. in para. 5.6 above; see also *Ansah* v. *Ansah* [1977] Fam. 138 and *Masich* v. *Masich* (1977) 7 Fam. Law 245.

expedited personal protection orders (but not exclusion orders) without any or on short notice.[10] Whilst general rules of court already exist in the High Court and county courts governing procedure for ex parte applications,[11] there are no rules in the magistrates' courts. One of our principal aims in undertaking this project has been to remove unnecessary distinctions between different courts and where possible, to give them uniform powers within a unified jurisdiction. We think this can be best achieved by providing an overall statutory framework which contains common principles and procedures with a standard test and have therefore made express provision for this in the draft Bill. The standard test would be that applied at present in the higher courts,[12] that the court should have a general discretion to grant orders where in all the circumstances it would be just and convenient to do so. Including this in the legislation has the further advantage of permitting some indication to be given of the special features which should be taken into account when the courts are dealing with ex parte applications in these cases, thus providing a degree of consistency between courts and also some guidance for the lay magistrates who will be called upon to exercise these powers. These factors will not be exclusive: the court should in each case take into account any other relevant circumstances. They are, however, cumulative, and any one of them might be decisive in a particular case.

5.8. In our view, the relevant factors should be the following:

(i) the risk of significant harm to the applicant or a child. This will cover cases in which there is evidence that the respondent has been violent towards or threatened violence to the applicant or a child, and there is a genuine risk that the violence will be repeated or the threat carried out unless an immediate order is made;

(ii) the likelihood of the applicant being deterred or prevented from pursuing the application. This will cover the category of cases mentioned by Ormrod L. J. in which the applicant is so terrified of the respondent that some protection is necessary to enable her to pursue her remedy, even though the remedy may not necessarily be urgent in itself; and

(iii) whether there is reasonable cause to believe that the respondent is aware of the proceedings but is deliberately evading service and the applicant or a child will be seriously prejudiced by the delay involved in serving the respondent or in effecting substituted service.

5.9 The usual solution to the problem of evasion of service is to resort to substituted service, but there are sometimes problems with this in the context of domestic violence. Substituted service is available in the High Court[13] and in the county courts,[14] but not in the magistrates' courts.[15] It will generally only be ordered when it is impracticable for the plaintiff to effect service in accordance with the rules and will not be ordered if the proceedings are not likely to reach the defendant or come to his knowledge if service is substituted. It may at times be difficult for an applicant to establish this likelihood, and effecting service may cause unacceptable delay.[16] A number of different respondents to our working paper stressed to us the problems caused by evasion of service. One firm of solicitors who undertake a great deal of domestic violence work said that the issue frequently caused difficulties and that great expense was often incurred in looking for respondents who kept "disappearing" when it was usually apparent that they were aware of the proceedings. Another consideration is that deliberate evasion of service is not infrequently used by respondents in domestic violence cases as a tactic to wear down the applicant's resolution by causing delay and making it even more difficult than it already is to pursue the proceedings against him. For

---

[10] Domestic Proceedings and Magistrates' Courts Act 1978, s.16(6); Magistrates' Courts (Matrimonial Proceedings) Rules 1980, r.19.

[11] e.g. R.S.C. 0.8, r.2; C.C.R. 0.13, r.1(3).

[12] Supreme Court Act 1981, s.37(1) and (2).

[13] R.S.C. 0.65, r.4.

[14] C.C.R. 0.7, r.8.

[15] Although modes of service are generally wider in magistrates' courts in that a summons may be effectively served not only by personal delivery but also by leaving it with some person at or sending it by post to the individual's last known or usual place of abode, (Magistrates' Courts Rules, 1981, r.99(1)), summonses under Domestic Proceedings and Magistrates' Courts Act 1978, ss.16 and 17 have to be served personally unless the court is satisfied by evidence on oath that prompt personal service of the summons is impracticable, (r.99(7)).

[16] In the High Court, substituted service of a document may be ordered if it appears to the court that it is impracticable for any reason to serve the document in the manner prescribed by the rules: R.S.C. 0. 65, r.4(1). But a note in the Supreme Court Practice 1991, para. 65/4/7, suggests as a guide in ordinary cases that an application should be made by affidavit after, inter alia, two calls at the respondent's residence on separate weekdays at reasonable hours, the second being by appointment by letter sent to the respondent giving not less than 2 clear day's notice and offering an opportunity of making a different appointment.

some applicants, this can be the last straw, and the proceedings may be withdrawn or abandoned. Most of these cases, but not all of them, will be covered by the factors mentioned in (i) or (ii) above and we are satisfied that evasion of service can cause sufficient difficulties to justify specifying it as a separate factor. In such circumstances, the balance of both justice and convenience may well be in favour of making an ex parte order with a short return date, the respondent being at liberty to apply.[17]

5.10 We accordingly *recommend* that the court should retain a general discretion to grant orders without giving the notice prescribed by rules of court to the respondent where in all the circumstances it would be just and convenient[18] but that there should also be a requirement to take the following factors into account:

(i) the risk of significant harm to the applicant or a child if the order is not made immediately;

(ii) whether it is likely that the applicant will be deterred or prevented from pursuing the application if an order is not made immediately; and

(iii) whether there is reason to believe that the respondent is aware of the proceedings but is deliberately evading service and the applicant or a child will be seriously prejuduced by the delay involved either in effecting service in proceedings in a magistrates' court or in any other case, in effecting substituted service.

Enforcement

(a) Powers of arrest

5.11 The Domestic Violence and Matrimonial Proceedings Act 1976 broke new ground by enabling the High Court or a county court to attach a power of arrest to an injunction which either restrains one party from using violence or contains an exclusion order.[19] Powers of arrest may also be attached to orders made in proceedings under the Domestic Proceedings and Magistrates' Courts Act 1978[20] in similar circumstances, although there are a number of minor differences between and uncertainties about the exact scope of these powers.[21] Under the present law, powers of arrest are regarded as relatively exceptional measures, they are normally subject to a time limit of three months[22] and tend to be attached to a minority of injunctions.[23]

5.12 In the working paper we suggested that the court should be able to attach a power of arrest to any order provided that the respondent had in fact caused actual bodily harm to the victim and the order specified exactly what breaches of the order would give rise to the power of arrest, unless in all the circumstances it appeared that the applicant or a child would be adequately protected without it.[24] Consultation revealed a considerable diversity of views on this subject, but there appeared to be three main options. Some respondents favoured the present law, considering that powers of arrest should be relatively exceptional. Others would allow powers of arrest to be attached in any case where there was a risk of future harm, but a few feared that if injunctions normally carried a power of arrest, there might be an increased reluctance to grant them. A third sizeable and varied group of

---

[17] There are other instances of procedures being adapted to allow ex parte orders to be made for what are, in effect, pressing policy reasons, e.g. Anton Piller orders which have been developed as a procedural device to protect and preserve certain items of evidence vital to the plaintiff's case from destruction by the defendant. The basic form of order requires the defendant to permit the plaintiff or his solicitor to enter the defendant's premises and seize, photograph or take copies of any documents or goods specified in the order. Orders can be obtained only in relation to existing or imminent proceedings, but without notice being given to the defendant and are designed to overcome the problem of the defendant frustrating the plaintiff's action by destroying illegal documents or goods as soon as he is alerted to the litigation.
[18] This reflects the existing position. See Courts and Legal Services Act 1990, Sched. 18, para. 21.
[19] Domestic Violence and Matrimonial Proceedings Act 1976, s.2(1).
[20] s.18(1).
[21] See, for examples, working paper No. 113, paras. 5.9–5.15.
[22] *Practice Note (Domestic Violence: Powers of Arrest)* [1981] 1 W.L.R. 27.
[23] In 1989, the last year for which figures are available, out of a total of 20,419 injunctions granted under Domestic Violence and Matrimonial Proceedings Act 1976, s. 1, powers of arrest were attached in 5,870 cases (29%). 3,421 injunctions with a power of arrest attached were granted in matrimonial proceedings and 748 powers of arrest were attached to existing injunctions, but there are no figures for the total number of matrimonial injunctions granted. Lord Chancellor's Department, *Judical Statistics Annual Report 1989*, (1990), Table 5.13, p. 61.
[24] See working paper No. 113, para. 6.64.

respondents[25] suggested that powers of arrest should generally be attached in cases where there had been violence or threatened violence.

5.13 We were impressed by the weight of informed opinion supporting this third main alternative, which, although details differed, proposed a presumption in favour of powers of arrest in cases where there has been violence and threatened violence. There are a number of advantages in this. A power of arrest is seen as a simple, immediate and inexpensive means of enforcement which underlines the seriousness of the breach to the offending party. It was felt that threatened violence should be included because it is wrong in principle that women and children should have to wait to be injured before the law can offer effective protection. However it could be wrong to provide for an absolutely automatic power of arrest as there may well be some cases in which it is inappropriate. We therefore *recommend* that where there has been violence or threatened violence the court should be required to attach a power of arrest to any specified provisions of an order in favour of any eligible applicant unless in all the circumstances the applicant or child will be adequately protected without such a power.

5.14 We do however see a case for differentiating between powers of arrest granted after an inter partes hearing and those granted ex parte. It must be appropriate to take a more stringent approach to the latter, as the court is being asked to grant a power of arrest against someone who has not yet had an opportunity of stating his case. We therefore *recommend* that in the case of ex parte orders, the court should not be under any obligation to attach a power of arrest but should be able to do so in cases where there has been actual or threatened violence, provided that it is also satisfied that there is a risk of significant harm to the applicant or a child if the power is not attached immediately. In all cases, the particular breach which will give rise to the operation of the power of arrest should be clearly specified.

(b) Warrants for arrest

5.15 Arguments in favour of attaching a power of arrest to an order where there has been no violence are less persuasive. The use of powers of arrest should be confined to serious cases where it is necessary to give extra weight to an order to drive home to the respondent the need to keep within its terms. Powers of arrest can be counter-productive and may exacerbate tensions unless they are reserved for cases in which they are shown to be necessary to prevent future injury. But applicants should have open to them methods of enforcement which are as effective as possible when breaches of non-molestation or occupation orders occur. Short of attaching a power of arrest, the High Court and county courts have at present no power to involve the police in the enforcement of orders made under the domestic violence legislation. Yet the police will already have been involved in incidents between the parties in many cases. They are the obvious agency to use and will generally be more effective at and experienced in handling domestic violence issues than either the High Court tipstaff or the county court bailiffs who are the only present resources of the higher courts in the event of committal proceedings. The magistrates' courts, however, have a useful power to involve the police, as they may issue an arrest warrant on application where there are reasonable grounds for believing that the respondent has disobeyed an order.[26] We *recommend* that this power to issue arrest warrants should be extended to the High Court and county courts.

(c) Remand

5.16 Magistrates' courts also have power to remand a person arrested pursuant to a power of arrest, either in custody or on bail, pending proceedings for committal or breach.[27] The higher courts have no such power at present, although since the working paper was

---

[25] Including the Magistrates' Association, Women's Aid Federation, Rights of Women, the Institute of Legal Executives, the Children's Legal Centre, the Association of Women Solicitors, the Law Society, the Family Law Bar Association, the National Council for One Parent Families, the Association of Chief Police Officers and the Metropolitan Police.

[26] Domestic Proceedings and Magistrates' Courts Act, 1978, s.18(4). This power was given to magistrates in 1978 because they had no powers of committal for contempt and it was considered unlikely that the existing enforcement machinery in section 54 of the Magistrates' Courts Act 1952 would include power to issue a warrant for arrest. Some reinforcement of magistrates' powers was therefore considered necessary in cases where the applicant or a child may have suffered physical injury and be at risk of a further attack. The power does not apply if there is already a power of arrest attached to the order. If arrested, the respondent can then be remanded on bail or in custody pending proceedings being taken for breach of the order under section 63(3) of the Magistrates' Courts Act 1980 either on complaint or of the court's own motion, (Contempt of Court Act 1981, s.17).

[27] Magistrates' Courts Act 1980, ss.128, 129.

published, the Court of Appeal has overturned received wisdom that the courts have no power to adjourn committal proceedings. It has held that when an arrested person is brought before the judge, the court is not bound either to release him or commit him for contempt, but can instead adjourn for further evidence to be adduced.[28] On consultation, an overwhelming majority of respondents were in favour of our proposal to extend the magistrates' power of remand to the High Court and county courts. We consider that such a development would be desirable, notwithstanding the recent recognition of a power to adjourn particularly because there may well be a need to remand in custody or on bail. It is generally preferable in principle that all courts should have the same powers, which, it is to be hoped, would be exercised consistently. A power of remand would give greater security and could benefit both parties by allowing them time to decide how they want to proceed. We therefore *recommend* that a power to remand, similar to that which the magistrates already have, should be extended to the High Court and county courts. In the draft Bill we have simply sought to repeat, for the higher civil courts, the regime already existing in the magistrates' courts, without reviewing its detailed operation.

5.17 In their response, the Council of Her Majesty's Circuit Judges drew attention to the desirability of a power to remand the respondent for medical examination in the not inconsiderable number of cases where it seems that the arrested person may be suffering from mental ill-health. The magistrates' courts already have a power to remand for medical reports[29] and we *recommend* that a similar power be extended to the High Court and county courts. We also *recommend* that the provisions of section 35 of the Mental Health Act 1983 (which gives the courts power to remand an accused or convicted person to hospital for medical reports) be extended to allow the court to use it to deal with someone arrested for breach of a non-molestation or occupation order.[30]

Third parties' standing to apply

5.18 In several Australian states, the police have standing to apply for civil remedies under the domestic violence legislation.[31] There appear to be variations between states in the extent to which the police use this power but it is generally regarded as a useful and valuable provision.[32] Such a power is seen as having a number of advantages. In many cases, the victim is in a state of helplessness because of the violence and is unable to take any initiative herself. Giving this power to the police removes the burden of taking action from her, reduces the scope for further intimidation by the perpetrator and leads to far fewer cases being withdrawn. In addition, it is seen to be in the police's interests to take steps to stop further violence because this will eventually lighten their workload.[33] The fact that the police are initiating the proceedings also has the beneficial effect of bringing home to the respondent the seriousness of the matter and giving civil proceedings the "weight" they can lack in the eyes of some of the less law abiding members of society. There is also an argument that having the power to bring civil proceedings encourages the police to upgrade the importance of domestic violence and become more aware and sensitive in relation to it. They may also be more prepared to arrest for breach if they themselves have initiated the proceedings and obtained the order.

5.19 Giving such powers to the police would be an innovation in this country and certain reservations were expressed on consultation. Respondents were concerned in principle about the intrusion of the police into the civil law, the manner in which they might exercise their powers and the degree of attention which would be paid to the wishes and interests of the

---

[28] *Roberts* v. *Roberts* [1991] 1 F.L.R. 294; see also *Practice Direction* [1991] 1 W.L.R. 278.

[29] Magistrates' Courts Act 1980, s.10(3).

[30] Such extension would be without the limitation imposed by Contempt of Court Act 1981, s.14(4A), which restricts the application of section 35 of the 1983 Act in contempt proceedings to a "person who could be committed to prison", and accordingly requires a finding of contempt to be made before an order can be made under s.35; in other proceedings no preliminary finding of guilt is necessary.

[31] In New South Wales, the Crimes Act 1900, s.562C; in South Australia, the Justices Act 1921, s.99(2); in Western Australia, the Justices Act 1902, s.172(2); in Victoria, the Crimes (Family Violence) Act 1987, s.7; in the Australian Capital Territories, Domestic Violence Ordinance 1986, s.5.

[32] *The Australian Law Reform Commission, Domestic Violence*, Report No. 30, (1986), p. 41, the Commission was not able to determine why different patterns had emerged, but a study carried out in South Australia in 1985 showed that approximately 97% of orders were applied for by the police, whereas in New South Wales, the police were more reluctant to use the power. But it seems that in New South Wales the police are making greater use of the power as they become more familiar with it. In 1986 only 5% of apprehended violence orders were initiated by the police, whereas in 1987, the police initiated 20% of a much greater number of orders. See D. Chappell and H. Strang, "Domestic Violence—Findings and Recommendations of the National Committee on Violence" [1990] Australian J. Fam. L. 211.

[33] *Ibid.*

woman involved. Some people considered that indiscriminate and insensitive use of such powers could place many women in a worse position than at present, whereas others thought such powers would be largely ineffective because the police would be reluctant to become involved. There is also an argument (contrary to that expressed above) that introducing the possibility of the police taking action under the civil law might have the undesirable effect of discouraging prosecutions in cases in which they might otherwise be brought.

5.20 Whilst expressing caution, police respondents did not specifically oppose such a power, although they had concerns about the need for police intervention in other than emergency situations and about resource implications. The Metropolitan Police accepted the need for some victims to have support and assistance but suggested that an alternative body might provide this. But the provision of support and assistance is rather different to actually taking legal proceedings on behalf of someone else and it is difficult to think of an alternative body which could fulfil the latter role. Often, the police will already be involved and will have witnessed the aftermath of incidents of domestic violence or abuse, if not the incident itself. They are accustomed to handling these problems and to participating in court proceedings. The police also represent the role of society in protecting individuals from violence and abuse. It would be difficult to ensure that other categories of representatives were always acting from proper motives and with the interests of the victim at heart. Extending standing to other groups would be a major innovation for which we think that there is on balance insufficient justification at the moment. Extending it to the police would, however, have advantages. It would give the police greater flexibility in the way they respond to domestic crises without putting them under any obligation to apply for civil remedies or deterring criminal proceedings if these are more appropriate. We therefore *recommend* that where they have been involved in an incident of molestation or actual or threatened violence, or its aftermath, the police should have power to apply for civil remedies on behalf of the victim.

5.21 We envisage this operating in the following way. The police would have power to apply for a civil order where they had attended at or following an incident of molestation or violence, and had reasonable cause to believe that such abuse had occurred. They could then apply for a non-molestation or occupation order against the aggressor, provided that the people concerned fell within the categories of associated persons within these proposals,[34] and provided that the police consider this would be an appropriate course of action for them to take. There would be no obligation on the police to take civil proceedings, but the option would be available either as an alternative to or in addition to criminal proceedings.

5.22 The question of whether the victim's consent should be necessary before the police bring civil proceedings has caused us some difficulty. On one view of the matter, it can be said that for a non-molestation or occupation order to be effective, the active co-operation of the victim is required. It would be a waste of the court's time and the resources of the police if, for example, the police were to apply for orders against the victim's wishes, only to find that when an occupation order was granted, the victim immediately invited the assailant back home. Also, it is in most cases appropriate for the woman concerned to have control over the proceedings brought on her behalf. There is otherwise a risk that legal procedures will perpetuate rather than alleviate the powerlessness often induced by repeated violence. On the other hand, requiring the victim's consent could be seen as undermining many of the reasons suggested above for giving the police power to bring the proceedings, as the victim would then be open to threats and intimidation on this account. Some victims might be prepared passively to co-operate in proceedings initiated by the police, although they dare not positively authorise such proceedings or institute proceedings themselves. It may be possible on some occasions to obtain a non-molestation order without the co-operation of the victim, if, for example, clear evidence is available from relatives or social workers. Automatically to assume that nothing can be done unless the victim co-operates produces the unfortunate paradox that the woman who has been so terrorised that she dare not take any steps to protect herself is the one person deprived of any protection.

5.23 There is a third alternative, to require the police to consult the woman concerned and take account of her views. This should give the victim a significant degree of influence over the conduct of proceedings by the police, but does not make her consent or approval the decisive factor in determining whether or not civil proceedings are issued. The police could then take action where the victim asks them to and would be in a better position to

---

[34] i.e. the categories set out in paras. 3.26 and 4.9 above.

obtain the necessary information to enable them to distinguish cases where the woman genuinely does not want civil proceedings issued (and to do so would be a waste of everyone's time), from cases in which she does want some action taken against her assailant but does not dare to initiate or authorise it directly. The police could also properly emphasise to the assailant that the decision to issue civil proceedings is out of the victim's hands. It would also be possible, as an additional safeguard, to provide that when proceedings are taken by the police, the court should take account of the wishes of the victim before making any order. This would ensure that the court was made aware of any change in the victim's views between the time of the police intervention and the date of the court hearing. We accordingly *recommend* that the police should be under a duty to consult the victim and to take account of her views in deciding whether to issue and how to conduct any civil proceedings. In cases where proceedings are brought by the police, the court should have a duty to take the victim's views into account before making any order.

PART VI

OTHER ISSUES

Transfer of tenancies

6.1 On or after granting a decree of divorce, nullity or judicial separation, the court has power, under section 7 of and Schedule 1 to the Matrimonial Homes Act 1983[1] to transfer a statutory, protected, secure or assured tenancy from one spouse to the other or from them both to one alone. There is, however, no power to do this in the case of cohabitants and this has, as we have already discussed,[2] led to difficulties in some situations. These have been felt most acutely in cases such as *Ainsbury* v. *Millington*[3] where deadlock arises as a result of neither joint tenant being prepared to agree to the transfer to the other or to determine the tenancy so that it can be regranted to one alone.

6.2 In Scotland, the courts have power to transfer tenancies between cohabitants who are joint tenants and also where a non-entitled cohabitant has been granted occupation rights.[4] We suggested in the working paper that a similar power should be introduced in this country.[5] On consultation, a substantial majority of respondents were in favour of the courts having power to transfer tenancies between cohabitants when their relationship has broken down. It was felt that this would remove the present discrimination against cohabitants in England and Wales (as compared with those in Scotland); would give the courts wider powers to ensure that children were properly housed; and would assist local authorities in discharging their responsibilities to people who would otherwise be homeless or be stranded for a long period of time in unsuitable accommodation whilst awaiting rehousing. The few respondents who expressed reservations based these not upon the effect of the proposal, but upon the need to explore more fully the general legal status of cohabitants before giving the court such a power.

6.3 Our conclusions on this subject have been influenced by several other considerations. Most affected tenancies are joint tenancies of a family sized home granted to the couple concerned by the local authority for the purpose of providing a home for them and their children. It is likely that the parties themselves understood that the property would be used as their joint home and the home of their children, and it might reasonably be said to have been in their contemplation that if their relationship foundered, only one of them would remain there, probably with the children. Where cohabitants are joint owners, the court takes account of the underlying purpose for which the trust was created, which, where the property in question is a family home, may often be the provision of such a home. Although there are conflicting dicta in the Court of Appeal about the precise effect that the continuing need of young children for a home should have upon general principles,[6] there is no dispute that their interests are an important factor to be taken into account in deciding the outcome of an application for sale. In consequence, it can be persuasively argued that the courts would, in an appropriate case, hold that the provision of a home for the children had been a primary or underlying purpose of the trust and refuse to order a sale unless alternative accommodation was available for them.[7] The transfer of a tenancy can in some respects be preferable to an indefinite ouster from the tenant's point of view as he will at least then be relieved of any ongoing liability for the payment of rent.

6.4 These parallels are less close in the case of a sole tenancy, at least if it was granted to one of the parties before their relationship began. However, there are bound to be cases in which the analogy is still valid, for example where one party moved in with a sole tenant (perhaps relinquishing a tenancy to do so), in circumstances which suggest a common intention that the sole tenant's property should henceforth be their joint family home. Moreover, some sole tenancies may still be granted to existing families, where it is the intention of all concerned that it be used as a home for them all.

---

[1] There is also a possibility of some tenancies being transferred in proceedings ancillary to divorce, nullity or judicial separation under Matrimonial Causes Act 1973, s.24(1).

[2] See paras. 2.18–2.20 above.

[3] [1986] 1 All E.R. 73. See para. 2.19 above.

[4] Matrimonial Homes (Family Protection) (Scotland) Act 1981, ss.18(3) and 13.

[5] See working paper No. 113, para. 6.6.

[6] cf. *Rawlings* v. *Rawlings* [1964] P. 398, 419, *per* Salmon L.J., *Burke* v. *Burke* [1974] 1 W.L.R. 1063, 1068, *per* Lawton L.J., *Williams* v. *Williams* [1976] Ch. 278 and *Re Citro* [1991] Ch. 142 with *Burke* v. *Burke* [1974] 1 W.L.R. 1063, 1067, *per* Buckley L.J. and *Re Holliday* (*A Bankrupt*) [1981] Ch. 405, 417, *per* Goff L.J., 421, *per* Buckley L.J.

[7] S. M. Cretney and J. M. Masson, *Principles of Family Law*, (5th. ed.), (1990), p. 261.

6.5 A further relevant consideration is the introduction by the Family Law Reform Act 1987[8] of a power for the court to order the transfer or settlement of property between unmarried parents for the benefit of their children. The purpose of this amendment was to place the children of unmarried parents on an equal footing with the children of married parents so far as the powers of the court to make financial provision are concerned. The Court of Appeal has recently held that this power does enable the court to order one parent to transfer his rights in a joint tenancy of a council house to the other parent for the benefit of their children.[9] However, although this is clearly an extension of the court's powers to resolve the problems arising on the breakdown of non-marital relationships, there are a number of potential difficulties which render it unlikely that this provision could provide a complete solution to the *Ainsbury* v. *Millington*[10] problem.[11] There is the difficulty that (with three exceptions) neither a secure periodic tenancy or a fixed term secure tenancy granted on or after 5 November 1982 is capable of being assigned.[12] Transfers may sometimes be possible by virtue of the exception in section 91(3)(c) of the Housing Act 1985 which permits assignment in favour of a person who would have been qualified to succeed the tenant had the tenant died immediately before the assignment.[13] Orders under Schedule 1 of the Children Act 1989 (in which the Family Law Reform Act power is now to be found) do not, however, automatically come within these exceptions and accordingly it seems likely that any purported transfer under that provision would be ineffective and unenforceable unless it also satisfied the conditions in section 91(3)(c).[14] In such circumstances, it is unlikely that the court would be prepared to entertain an application. It is also possible that if the tenancy is not capable of being assigned, the court could take the view that it was not "property" for the purposes of the power to order transfer.[15] However, the real problem with this as a solution to the *Ainsbury* v. *Millington* problem is that it is a contrivance. The power to transfer was designed to enable the court to provide for the children of unmarried parents and not specifically to do justice between the parents themselves. Although the courts have power to make property or capital settlements for the benefit of children on divorce, they have generally been reluctant to do so.[16] There must be a likelihood that a similar attitude would prevail in relation to the transfer of tenancies. Further, as children cannot hold a legal estate in land,[17] this transfer would in any event have to be to the parent for their benefit. If the merits of the case warrant a transfer, it would be less artificial as well as more effective to order a transfer to the adult outright.

6.6 These considerations have led us to the firm conclusion that the power to transfer tenancies at present contained in the Matrimonial Homes Act 1983 should be extended to cohabitants, whether they are joint tenants or whether one party is a sole tenant and the other is non-entitled. We therefore *recommend* accordingly. There would, of course, be no entitlement to such a transfer in any particular situation. The court would simply have power to make such an order if the merits of the case justified it. If they did not, it would not be done.

---

[8] s.32 and Sched. 1 inserted a new s.11B in the Guardianship of Minors Act 1971, now the Children Act 1989, Sched. 1, para. 1. This enacted the recommendation made in our report, *Illegitimacy*, Law Com. No. 118, (1982), para. 6.6.

[9] *K.* v. *K., The Times,* February 21, 1992.

[10] [1986] 1 All E.R. 73.

[11] See paras. 2.19 and 6.1 above.

[12] Housing Act 1985, s.91(1). The three exceptions provided under s.91(3) are: assignments by way of exchange under s.92; assignments under s.24 Matrimonial Causes Act 1973; and assignment to a member of the tenant's family who would be qualified to succeed the tenant under the succession provisions in s.87.

[13] Qualification is defined in ss.87 and 88. Unless the tenant (before the assignment) was himself a successor, any member of his family who resided with him during the previous twelve months qualifies. The relationship is defined in s.113, to include unmarried partners who live together as husband and wife, step children and illegitimate children.

[14] There are other provisions of the housing legislation which similarly refer to orders under the Matrimonial Causes Act 1973 but not to orders under the Children Act 1989 (e.g. Housing Act 1985, ss.39, 88, 89, 90, 101, 160, 171B). This discrepancy between orders made for or for the benefit of the children of married parents under the Matrimonial Causes Act 1973, s.24 and orders made for or for the benefit of the children of unmarried parents under the Children Act 1989, Sched. 1, para. 1 is clearly unsatisfactory and contrary to the non-discriminatory policy of the 1987 Act. It could, however, be eliminated in any of three ways: (i) by excluding orders for the benefit of children from the references to orders made under s.24 of the 1973 Act in the Housing Acts; (ii) by adding to the Housing Acts references to orders made under Sched. 1, para. 1 of the 1989 Act; or (iii) by a careful scrutiny of each of the relevant provisions of the Housing Acts to see whether and how orders for the benefit of children ought to be included.

[15] *Hale* v. *Hale* [1975] 1 W.L.R. 931, 937; Megarry, *The Rent Acts,* (11th ed.), Vol. 1, pp. 252–253.

[16] *Chamberlain* v. *Chamberlain* [1973] 1 W.L.R. 1557; *Lilford (Lord)* v. *Glynn* [1979] 1 W.L.R. 78.

[17] Law of Property Act 1925, s.19.

6.7 Under the present law, remarriage bars a former spouse from applying for the transfer of a tenancy under the Matrimonial Homes Act 1983.[18] The question arises whether any similar provision should be applied in relation to cohabitants. Whilst it seems in principle undesirable to make a distinction between former spouses and former cohabitants in this respect, and particularly to place former cohabitants in what might be regarded as a better position than former spouses; there are serious objections to introducing a similar bar for former cohabitants on subsequent marriage. The main difficulty is that there is no clear cut-off point when cohabitation ends in the same way that a decree absolute terminates a marriage. Also, most people who divorce have the benefit of legal advice in respect of ancillary matters, and will, if necessary, either have applied for the transfer of a tenancy in ancillary proceedings or under the Matrimonial Homes Act 1983, before there is any question of remarriage. There is no similar trigger to prompt cohabitants to make an application. Frequently they will not have had legal advice when their relationship breaks down and so will be unaware of their rights and any restrictions on them. They will also generally be in a position to marry someone else almost immediately. To cut off, on subsequent marriage, the right to apply for the transfer of a tenancy could lead to cases of considerable hardship. It should also be borne in mind that the jurisdiction to grant the transfer is discretionary and a cohabitant who had subsequently married would only succeed in an application if it were justified on the merits. Accordingly, we think that a distinction between former spouses and former cohabitants is justifiable in these circumstances and that it would on balance be wrong to introduce a bar for cohabitants on subsequent marriage.

6.8 The question then arises whether it would be appropriate to have statutory guidelines, or whether the exercise of this extended power should be left entirely to the discretion of the court. In Scotland, section 13 of the Matrimonial Homes (Family Protection) (Scotland) Act 1981 provides that the court shall have regard to all the circumstances of the case including such matters as the conduct of the parties in relation to each other and otherwise, their needs and financial resources, the needs of the children, the suitability of the applicant to be a tenant and the applicant's ability to perform the obligations of a tenant. One argument against statutory guidelines is the fact that, at present, the Matrimonial Homes Act 1983 does not contain any. If they are to be introduced, there seems to be no good reason for distinguishing between spouses and cohabitants in this respect and we think that they should apply to both. On balance, we consider that it would be helpful to provide some guidance upon the factors the court should take into account in order to reach a fair and just solution as to which partner should have the tenancy in the future.

6.9 In cases under section 30 of the Law of Property Act 1925, the courts take into account the underlying basis of the trust, that is, the circumstances in which it was established and its general purpose—was it the provision of a home for the parties and their children? This seems an equally important factor here. Other relevant factors would be the parties' various needs and resources identified in relation to occupation orders and their respective suitability as tenants. We accordingly *recommend* that new statutory criteria should be introduced directing the court to have regard to all the circumstances of the case and in particular

(i) the circumstances in which the tenancy was granted to either or both parties, or as the case requires, the circumstances in which either or both of them became tenant under the tenancy;

(ii) the various needs and resources previously defined in relation to regulatory occupation orders[19] and in the case of non-entitled cohabitants the additional factors previously defined in relation to them;[20] and

(iii) the respective suitability of the parties as tenants.

6.10 In Scotland, in addition to the provision of guidelines, section 13(1) and (9) of the Matrimonial Homes (Family Protection) (Scotland) Act 1981 allows the court to order payment by the transferee to the transferor of such compensation as seems just and reasonable in all the circumstances of the case. However, when the court exercises this power, it is prohibited from taking into account the loss of the "right to buy" under the Housing (Scotland) Act 1987 in assessing compensation. The Matrimonial Homes Act 1983 has no equivalent provisions. Again, if they are to be introduced, there seems to be no good reason

---

[18] Schedule 1, para. 7.
[19] See para. 4.33 above and clause 7(5)(a), (b) and (c) of the draft Bill.
[20] See para. 4.13 above and clause 9(4)(a) and (b) of the draft Bill.

for distinguishing between spouses and cohabitants in principle, although spouses' mutual obligations of support might tend to make compensation less appropriate in their case than in the case of cohabitants. The object of a compensation order would be to compensate a tenant for the loss of his tenancy. Relevant criteria would include the degree of financial loss suffered, the needs and resources of the parties and their ability to pay and also any actual or potential liability to maintain the other party or any child concerned. Compensation would not be a means of providing cohabitants with maintenance or capital payments. Although a statutory tenancy is a personal right and not a property right,[21] we think that it would still be appropriate to leave the question of compensation to the discretion of the court. Where the tenancy is of no real market value, it may still be right to grant compensation for removal expenses or the provision of a deposit for a tenancy in the private sector.

6.11 Although the probability is that a compensation payment would be appropriate only in a very small number of cases, we think that power to make such an order would nevertheless be valuable. Some of our respondents expressed concern about loss of the "right to buy" under the housing legislation. We appreciate the reasons for excluding this from consideration in Scotland, in that this is designed to avoid the risk of a wife who obtains a transfer of a local authority tenancy having to pay compensation to her husband (the original tenant) for the potential capital gain he might have realised if he had purchased and then sold the property. However, we feel that the possibility of taking this into account should not be specifically excluded, as there may be a few cases in which it is appropriate. One of the most important factors in assessing any compensation payment will be the place occupied by such a transfer in any overall settlement between the parties. In the case of spouses, who have mutual obligations of support, the payment of compensation will be less likely than in the case of cohabitants where no such obligations exist.

6.12 We therefore *recommend* that whenever the court makes an order for the transfer of a tenancy it should have power to direct the payment of compensation by the transferee to the transferor. In deciding whether to exercise this power, the court should have regard to all the circumstances of the case and in particular to

(i) the financial loss which would be suffered by the transferor;

(ii) the financial needs and financial resources of the parties; and

(iii) the financial obligations which the parties have or are likely to have in the foreseeable future, including financial obligations to each other or to any relevant child.

Methods of dealing with property disputes

6.13 Section 17 of the Married Women's Property Act 1882 provides a summary procedure for married couples whereby claims to a beneficial interest in property to which only one partner is legally entitled may be determined. This procedure has been extended to couples whose marriage has been dissolved or annulled[22] and to couples whose engagement to marry has been ended,[23] provided proceedings are brought within three years of those events. However, cohabitants who have not been engaged to marry cannot use the procedure. Orders may be made in respect of property which is no longer in the other's possession and can extend to the proceeds of sale and to other property representing the original.[24] Once the court has declared the respective interests of the partners, it may make such order as it thinks fit, including an order for sale.[25] This procedure is available in the county courts without the financial restrictions applicable to ordinary property actions. As an order under section 17 is not capable of interfering with the parties' respective property rights under the general law, no breach or extension of principle would be involved.

6.14 We suggested in the working paper that consideration should be given to allowing more cases involving the property of cohabitants to be begun and heard in the county courts where they might be consolidated with molestation and occupation cases.[26] Since then, the problem of limited financial jurisdiction has eased somewhat as a result of the Courts and

---

[21] *Keeves* v. *Dean* [1924] 1 K.B. 685; *Roe* v. *Russell* [1928] 2 K.B. 117; *Jessamine Investment Co.* v. *Schwartz* [1978] Q.B. 264.

[22] Matrimonial Property and Proceedings Act 1970, s.39.

[23] Law Reform Act 1970, s.2.

[24] Matrimonial Causes (Property and Maintenance) Act 1958, s.7.

[25] *Ibid.*, s.7(7).

[26] See working paper No. 113, para. 6.9.

Legal Services Act 1990.[27] In consequence, more property disputes between cohabitants are likely to be begun and heard in the county courts, but there will still be many cases in which an extension of the section 17 summary procedure to cohabitants would be beneficial. In the first place, the value of the property concerned will often be far in excess of £50,000 and, even if, because of the complexity of the issues, a case had to be transferred to the High Court, the procedure would still be quicker, simpler and cheaper than an ordinary action. It would also avoid the problems which arise at present in determining whether or not a couple were "engaged".[28] There is no particular logic in allowing the procedure to be used by an engaged couple who may never have lived together in the property but denying it to people who did live there as husband and wife. On consultation, a substantial majority of respondents who commented on this issue were firmly in favour of extending the section 17 procedure to cohabitants, and we accordingly *recommend* that it should be extended to allow cohabitants to apply for an order within three years of ceasing to live together as husband and wife.

Ouster orders for the protection of children

6.15 During the debates in Parliament which led to the passage of the Children Act 1989, considerable support was given to the possibility of ousting an abuser or suspected abuser from the home instead of having to remove the child,[29] but the question was not finally resolved. In Appendix A of the working paper, we raised this issue of ouster orders for the protection of children and suggested four possible approaches which might be considered.[30] One of these involved giving the court specific power to accept a voluntary undertaking to leave the property as opposed to making an ouster order. Respondents were divided upon the desirability of undertakings. Superficially, they are attractive. They allow the courts to accept the offer of a solution which will allow the child to remain undisturbed in the home for a short period while further investigations are made. The threat of sanctions for breach of an undertaking is the same as for an order, and the child can still be subsequently removed for his protection if this seems necessary. However, applications for emergency protection orders will invariably be made in the absence of the respondent and the proceedings would therefore have to be adjourned in order to arrange for the people concerned to attend. This could be dangerous for the child in a genuine emergency where the grounds for making an emergency protection order appear satisfied at the initial hearing. Also, if the aim of providing for ouster is to ensure that the child is spared the trauma of removal from home, a power of arrest is a better way of achieving this than the threat of subsequent sanctions. The parent looking after the child at home will have little incentive to report a breach of the undertaking if the only real sanction is the instant removal of the child. Further, it is generally considered that to attach a power of arrest to a voluntary undertaking would be a contradiction in terms as this would negative the conciliatory effect that undertakings are supposed to have. Therefore, although there is nothing to stop a higher court accepting an undertaking instead of making an order, we see little advantage in any extension of the present practice.

6.16 However, a power to oust an abuser or suspected abuser received much support in principle on consultation. There are obviously cases where a child needs immediate and guaranteed protection from risk of serious harm which can only be given by removal from home. There are other cases where instant removal is not obviously the answer, but there are serious concerns and it is difficult to know whether the trauma to the child of a hasty or unjustified removal will be greater than the hazards of leaving him at home pending further investigations. Sudden removal from home, whatever its deficiencies, always carries some risk to the child's welfare, varying with the age of the child and how the removal is done. In a few cases, there may be good reason to believe that the child can be properly safeguarded from harm if one of the adults is removed, at least until the matter can be properly investigated and the facts discovered. A further advantage of legislating is that it appears that some local authorities are already inducing suspected abusers to leave, rather

---

[27] Article 2(1)(a) of the High Court and County Courts Jurisdiction Order 1991 (made pursuant to ss.1 and 20 of the Courts and Legal Services Act 1990) which came into force on 1 July 1991, abolishes the previous financial limits on the jurisdiction of the county court in various property actions under Law of Property Act 1925, including those under s.30.

[28] e.g. many cohabitants do plan to marry in the future when they are free to do so. Can it be said that they are engaged?

[29] *Official Report* (H.C.), Standing Committee B, 25 May 1989, cols. 325–329.

[30] See working paper No. 113, Appendix A. The four options suggested were: hearing care and private law proceedings together; allowing local authority applications for private law remedies; accepting undertakings in emergency protection cases; and giving the court power to make ouster and non-molestation orders in proceedings for emergency protection, care and supervision proceedings.

than have the children removed, and this would provide a way of regularising and controlling the practice.[31] A diversity of views was expressed upon the preferred approach, or combination of approaches, but the majority of respondents shared our provisional view that such a power should be part of the child protection scheme in Parts IV and V of the Children Act 1989.

6.17 Hence, it would simply be an alternative means to the end sought by making an emergency protection order[32] or an interim care order,[33] under which the child can be removed from home for a short time. There was no support for its use as a long term alternative to a care order. In the short term, the needs of the child can take precedence over other considerations, but in the longer term considerations of property rights and the balance of hardship between adults must play a part. As one respondent put it: to have a long term ouster order would be tantamount to imposing a particular form a family relationship over a period of months which might simply be unsustainable in the context of a volatile and uncertain family situation. If it is in the child's long term interests for an ouster order to be continued instead of a care order being made, it would be more appropriate for the non-abusing parent to apply for a private law remedy against the abuser.[34] We therefore *recommend* that the Children Act 1989 should be amended to give the court power to make a short-term emergency ouster order for the protection of children.

6.18 We asked in the working paper whether the power should be an alternative to an emergency protection order or an interim care order, or a supplement to it. Respondents' views on this were divided, but we have been persuaded in favour of the latter. If the child is to be properly protected the local authority (or other applicant for an emergency protection order) must be in a position to remove the child immediately should the consent and co-operation of the caring parent be withdrawn; should the caring parent be found to be in collusion with the abuser; or should the abuser be found to be a different person living in the household. We accordingly *recommend* that the court should have power, on making an emergency protection order or an interim care order, also to make an order excluding a named individual from the child's home.

6.19 We were originally concerned at the risk that families might "lose both ways", in the sense of having both the suspected abuser and the child removed, if it were possible for the applicant to enforce an emergency protection order by removing the child without having to prove that the adult had breached the order by re-entering the home. However, some safeguard is provided by section 44(5)(a) of the 1989 Act, which provides that an applicant for an emergency protection order shall only remove a child in order to safeguard his welfare. If there has been no breach of the ouster order and no other relevant change of circumstances, the removal of the child would not be necessary in order to safeguard his welfare. There is no equivalent provision for an interim care order, and even if there were, the ouster order would still be in effect after the child had been removed. However, the point can be met by a provision that if the applicant or local authority places the child outside the family home, the ouster order should automatically lapse. We therefore *recommend* that if the local authority (or other applicant in the case of an emergency protection order)[35] places the child outside the home, the ouster order should lapse automatically.

6.20 Since we propose that an ouster order should be supplementary to an emergency protection order or an interim care order, it follows that an ouster order should be made only if the criteria for making these other orders are satisfied.[36] That is, there should be a two stage process. The court should first consider whether an emergency protection order or an interim care order should be granted. If it decides that such an order should be made, it should then decide whether or not the additional criteria for making an ouster order are fulfilled. These criteria should cover two main areas. First, the order should be made only if there is reasonable cause to believe that the likelihood of harm to the child will not arise if the named person is removed from the household. Secondly, there must be another parent

---

[31] Local authorities have power under the Children Act 1989, sched. 2, para. 5 to assist a suspected abuser living in the same premises as the child concerned to obtain alternative accommodation.

[32] Children Act 1989, s.44.

[33] *Ibid.*, s.38.

[34] Under our proposed scheme, it could alternatively be possible for the police to make an application on behalf of that parent in an appropriate case. See paras. 5.13–5.18.

[35] Anyone may apply for an emergency protection order and may thereby become responsible for the child; a local authority or other authorised person may apply for an interim care order, but the effect is always to make the local authority responsible for the child; Children Act 1989, ss.31(1), (9), 44(1), (4).

[36] Children Act 1989, ss.44(1) and 38(2) respectively.

or person in the household who is willing and able to provide reasonable care for the child. Several respondents suggested that the consent of the caring parent or other person should be required before the court makes an ouster order. Clearly, the co-operation of the person caring for the child is essential to the success of the order, and the provision of consent would be some indication to the court that this person is willing and able to provide reasonable care for the child in the meantime. However, we think that this should be determined objectively as a separate requirement by the court and not simply by the provision of that person's consent to the ouster. Otherwise, a non-abusing parent might come under heavy pressure from the other, perhaps to give consent in the hope of retaining the child at home, even though the child would not then be adequately protected. We accordingly *recommend* that before making an ouster order, the court should be required to consider all the circumstances and in particular, ensure that the following conditions are satisfied:

(i) that there is reasonable cause to believe that if a person is excluded from a dwelling-house in which the child lives, then the child will cease to suffer or cease to be likely to suffer significant harm; and

(ii) that another member of the household (whether a parent of the child or some other person) is able and willing to give to the child the care which it would be reasonable to expect a parent to give to him and that person consents to the order being made.

6.21 As the power to grant an ouster order would be merely supplementary to an emergency protection order or an interim care order, the court would be able to regulate contact, medical examination, treatment and assessment during the order in exactly the same ways as it does at present.[37] The parties would have the same right to challenge the order as they have to challenge the order to which it is supplementary.[38] The maximum duration of the ouster order would be the duration of the order to which it is supplementary, that is, eight days, extendable to a maximum of fifteen days for an emergency protection order[39] and basically eight weeks, extendable for four weeks at a time for an interim care order.[40] It should, however, be possible for the court to specify a shorter period or to abridge, extend or vary the period stated. We *recommend* accordingly.

6.22 In the working paper, we expressed the view that the attractions of ouster orders for the protection of children would be greatly increased if a power of arrest could be attached.[41] Those respondents who commented on this issue were generally in agreement. The particular benefit in attaching a power of arrest is that this provides an immediate protection for the child which would achieve the overall objective of avoiding the need to remove him from home. We therefore *recommend* that the court should have power to attach a power of arrest to an ouster order where this is necessary to protect the child from an immediate risk of significant harm. The criterion for exercising the power of arrest should be that the constable had reasonable cause to believe the person concerned to be in breach of the order.

---

[37] Children Act 1989, ss.38(6)–(8), 43, 44(6).
[38] *Ibid.*, ss.39 and 45(8).
[39] Children Act 1989, s.45(1)–(6).
[40] Children Act 1989, s.38(4) and (5).
[41] Working paper No. 113, Appendix A, para. 10.

PART VII

COLLECTED RECOMMENDATIONS

Part II—The Context

7.1 There should be two kinds of remedy, a non-molestation order and an occupation order, each with its own criteria and incidents, but capable of combination with one another and with other family law remedies in an appropriate case (para. 2.48).

Part III—Non-molestation Orders

Scope

7.2. The courts should continue to have power to grant protection against all forms of molestation, including violence. There should be no statutory definition of molestation (para. 3.1; clause 13).

7.3 The power to make non-molestation orders should be framed to make it clear that the order is a flexible one, capable of being tailored to the requirements of the particular case, but the court should also be able to prohibit molestation in its general form if the case so demands (para. 3.2; clause 13(4)).

Criteria

7.4 The court should have power to grant a non-molestation order where this is just and reasonable having regard to all the circumstances including the need to secure the health, safety or well-being of the applicant or a relevant child (para. 3.7; clause 13(3)).

Those who may be protected

7.5 A non-molestation order should be capable of being made between people who are associated with each other in any of the following ways:

(i) they are or have been married to each other;

(ii) they are cohabitants or former cohabitants;

(iii) they live or have lived in the same household, otherwise than merely by reason of one of them being the other's employee, tenant, lodger or boarder;

(iv) they are within a defined group of close relatives;

(v) they have at any time agreed to marry each other (whether or not that agreement has been terminated);

(vi) they have or have had a sexual relationship with each other (whether or not including sexual intercourse);

(vii) they are the parents of a child or, in relation to any child, are persons who have or have had parental responsibility for that child (whether or not at the same time); or

(viii) they are parties to the same family proceedings. (para. 3.26; clause 2).

Duration

7.6 Non-molestation orders should be capable of being made for any specified period or until further order (para. 3.28; clause 13(5)).

Part IV—Occupation Orders

7.7 The court should have power to make an occupation order with a variety of possible terms, either declaratory or regulatory. The declaratory orders would be those:

(i) declaring pre-existing occupation rights in the home;

(ii) extending statutory occupation rights beyond the termination of the marriage on divorce or death;

(iii) granting occupation rights in the home to non-entitled applicants.

The regulatory orders available would be those:

(iv) requiring one party to leave the home;

(v) suspending occupation rights and/or prohibiting one party from entering or re-entering the home, or part of the home;

(vi) requiring one party to allow the other to enter and/or remain in the home;

(vii) regulating the occupation of the home by either or both of the parties;

(viii) terminating occupation rights; and

(ix) excluding one party from a defined area in the vicinity of the home (para. 4.2; clause 7(1), (2), (3) and (4)).

7.8 Orders extending matrimonial home rights beyond termination of the marriage on death or divorce should be made in any case where the court considers it just and reasonable to do so (para. 4.3; clause 7(4) and (7)).

7.9 The court should have power to make an occupation order in respect of any dwelling-house which is, was or was intended to be the joint home of the parties (para. 4.4; clauses 7(1)(b), and 9(1)(a)).

7.10 An occupation order should be capable of being made

(a) in favour of entitled applicants, between people who are associated with one another in any of the following ways:

    (i) they are or have been married to each other;

    (ii) they are cohabitants or former cohabitants;

    (iii) they live or have lived in the same household, otherwise than merely by reason of one of them being the other's employee, tenant, lodger or boarder;

    (iv) they are within a defined group of close relatives;

    (v) they have at any time agreed to marry each other (whether or not that agreement has been terminated);

    (vi) they have or have had a sexual relationship with each other (whether or not including sexual intercourse);

    (vii) they are the parents of a child or, in relation to any child, are persons who have or have had parental responsibility for that child (whether or not at the same time); or

    (viii) they are parties to the same family proceedings; and

(b) in favour of non-entitled applicants, between people who are cohabitants, former cohabitants or former spouses (para. 4.9; clauses 1, 2, 7(1), 9(1) and 10(1)).

Non-entitled Applicants

7.11 Where a non-entitled applicant applies for an occupation order, the court should be required to consider the following qualifying criteria:

    (i) where the parties are cohabitants or former cohabitants, the nature of their relationship, the length of time during which they have lived together as husband and wife and whether there are children of both parties or for whom both parties have parental responsibility;

    (ii) where the parties are former cohabitants or former spouses, the length of time that has elapsed since the marriage was dissolved or annulled or since the parties ceased to live together; and

    (iii) the existence of any pending proceedings between the parties for financial provision or relating to the legal or beneficial ownership of the dwelling-house (para. 4.13; clause 9(4)).

7.12 Granting an occupation order in favour of a non-entitled applicant should have an effect similar to spouses' automatic rights of occupation under section 1 of the Matrimonial Homes Act 1983. The court should consider such applications in two stages. First, it should consider whether an occupation rights order should be granted taking into account the three factors in paragraph 7.14 below and the qualifying criteria relating to non-entitled applicants in paragraph 7.11 above. It should then decide whether, on the merits, a regulatory order ought to be made (para. 4.18; clause 9(2), (4), (5) and (6)).

7.13 Occupation rights granted to non-entitled applicants should be personal rights only and should not therefore be capable of registration as a charge against the property or be valid against a purchaser (para. 4.19).

Criteria for regulatory orders

7.14 The court should have power to grant a regulatory occupation order in any case after considering all the circumstances of the case and in particular the following factors:

    (i) the respective housing needs and resources of the parties and of any relevant child;

    (ii) the respective financial resources of the parties; and

(iii) the likely effect of any order, or of any decision by the court not to make an order, on the health, safety and well-being of the parties and of any relevant child.

However, the court should have a duty to make an order if it appears likely that the applicant or any relevant child will suffer significant harm if an order is not made and that such harm will be greater than the harm which the respondent or any relevant child will suffer if the order is made (para. 4.33; clauses 7(5) and (6) and 9(5) and (6)).

Duration

7.15 All occupation orders made between spouses, whether co-owners or not, and co-owners, whether cohabitants or not, should be capable of being made for any specified period or until further order (para. 4.36; clause 7(9)).

7.16 All occupation orders made in favour of non-entitled applicants should be limited up to six months in the first instance, with the possibility of renewal for up to six months at a time (para. 4.37; clause 9(8)).

Ancillary orders

7.17 The court should have power to make the following ancillary orders where it is just and reasonable to do so:

(i) to impose on either party obligations regarding the discharge of rent, mortgage instalments and other outgoings;

(ii) to impose on either party obligations as to the repair and maintenance of the home;

(iii) to order payments by the occupying party to an entitled non-occupier for that occupation;

(iv) to grant one party possession or use of furniture or other belongings.

In deciding whether an order is just and reasonable, the court should take into account the parties' financial resources and any financial obligations which they have or are likely to have in the foreseeable future including any financial obligations to each other or to any relevant child (para. 4.42; clause 12).

Part V—Common Matters

Jurisdiction

7.18 Non-molestation orders should be capable of being made:

(i) on application without any other proceedings having been issued; and

(ii) of the court's own motion or on application in any family proceedings.

Occupation orders should be capable of being made on application without any other proceedings being instituted or on application in any family proceedings (para. 5.3; clauses 11(2) and 13(1), (2)).

7.19 All courts should have the same jurisdiction to make non-molestation orders and occupation orders, but magistrates' courts should be required to transfer a case or to refuse jurisdiction if a dispute arises as to whether either party has a pre-existing legal, beneficial or statutory right to occupy the home unless it is unnecessary for this to be decided before dealing with the matter. As at present, jurisdiction to order the transfer of tenancies under what is now section 7 and Schedule 1 to the Matrimonial Homes Act 1983 should be restricted to the higher courts (para. 5.4; clause 23(3); Schedule 4, Part 1).

Emergencies—ex parte orders

7.20 The court should retain a general discretion to grant orders without giving the notice prescribed by rules of court to the respondent where in all the circumstances it would be just and convenient, but there should also be a requirement to take the following factors into account:

(i) the risk of significant harm to the applicant or a child if the order is not made immediately;

(ii) whether it is likely that the applicant will be deterred or prevented from pursuing the application if an order is not made immediately; and

(iii) whether there is reason to believe that the respondent is aware of the proceedings but is deliberately evading service and the applicant or a child will be seriously prejudiced by the delay involved either in effecting service in proceedings in a magistrates' court or, in any other case, in effecting substituted service (para. 5.10; clause 14).

Enforcement

7.21 Where there has been violence or threatened violence, the court should be required to attach a power of arrest to any specified provisions of an order in favour of any eligible applicant, unless in all the circumstances the applicant or any child will be adequately protected without such a power (para. 5.13; clause 15(2)).

7.22 In the case of ex parte orders, the court should not be under any obligation to attach a power of arrest, but should be able to do so in cases where there has been actual or threatened violence, provided that it is also satisfied that there is a risk of significant harm to the applicant or a child if the power is not attached immediately (para. 5.14; clause 15(3)).

7.23 The High Court and county courts should have power to issue arrest warrants (para. 5.15; clause 15(6) and (7)).

7.24 The High Court and county courts should have power to remand (para. 5.16; clause 15(8) and (9); Schedule 2).

7.25 The High Court and county courts should have power to remand for medical reports and the provisions of section 35 of the Mental Health Act 1983 should be extended to allow the court to remand to hospital someone arrested for breach of a non-molestation order or an occupation order (para. 5.17; clause 16).

Third parties' standing to apply

7.26 Where the police have been involved in an incident of molestation or actual or threatened violence, or its aftermath, they should have power to apply for civil remedies on behalf of the victim (para. 5.20; clause 17(1), (2)).

7.27 The police should be under a duty to consult the victim and take account of her views in deciding whether or not to issue and how to conduct civil proceedings. In cases where proceedings are brought by the police, the court should have a duty to take the victim's views into account before making an order (para. 5.23; clause 17(1)(c), (3)(a)).

Part VI—Other Issues

Transfer of tenancies

7.28 The power to transfer tenancies at present contained in the Matrimonial Homes Act 1983 should be extended to cohabitants whether they are joint tenants or whether one party is a sole tenant and the other is non-entitled (para. 6.6; clause 19; Schedule 4, para. 3).

7.29 Statutory criteria should be introduced directing the court to have regard to all the circumstances of the case and in particular

(i) the circumstances in which the tenancy was granted to either or both parties, or as the case requires, the circumstances in which either or both of them became tenant under the tenancy;

(ii) the various needs and resources previously defined in relation to regulatory occupation orders (see para. 7.14 above) and, in the case of non-entitled cohabitants, the additional factors previously defined in relation to them (see para. 7.11 above); and

(iii) the respective suitability of the parties as tenants (para. 6.9; Schedule 4, para. 5).

7.30 The court should have power to direct the payment of compensation by the transferee to the transferor whenever it makes an order for the transfer of a tenancy. In deciding whether to exercise this power, the court should have regard to all the circumstances of the case and in particular to

(i) the financial loss which would be suffered by the transferor;

(ii) the financial needs and financial resources of the parties; and

59

(iii) the financial obligations which the parties have or are likely to have in the foreseeable future including any financial obligations to each other or to any relevant child (para. 6.12; Schedule 4, para. 10).

Methods of dealing with property disputes

7.31 The summary procedure under section 17 of the Married Women's Property Act 1882 for determining claims to a beneficial interest in property to which only one partner is legally entitled should be extended to allow cohabitants to apply for an order within three years of ceasing to live together (para. 6.14; clause 21).

Ouster orders for the protection of children

7.32 The Children Act 1989 should be amended to give the court power to make a short-term emergency ouster order for the protection of children (para. 6.17; clause 18; Schedule 3).

7.33 The court should have power, on making an emergency protection order or an interim care order, also to make an order excluding a named individual from the child's home (para. 6.18; Schedule 3, paras. 1 and 3).

7.34 If the local authority (or other applicant for an interim care order) places the child outside the home, the ouster order should lapse automatically (para. 6.19; Schedule 3, paras. 1 and 3).

7.35 The court should be required to ensure that before making an ouster order, the following conditions are satisfied:
   (i) that there is reasonable cause to believe that if a person is excluded from a dwelling-house in which the child lives, then the child will cease to suffer or cease to be likely to suffer significant harm; and
   (ii) that another member of the household (whether a parent of the child or some other person) is able and willing to give to the child the care which it would be reasonable to expect a parent to give him and consents to the order being made (para. 6.20; Schedule 3, paras. 1 and 3).

7.36 The maximum duration of the ouster order would be the duration of the order to which it is supplementary, but it should be possible for the court to specify a shorter period or to abridge, extend or vary the period stated (para. 6.21; Schedule 3, paras. 1 and 4).

7.37 The court should have power to attach a power of arrest to an ouster order where this is necessary to protect the child from an immediate risk of significant harm (para. 6.22; Schedule 3, paras. 1 and 3).

(*Signed*) PETER GIBSON, *Chairman*
TREVOR M. ALDRIDGE
JACK BEATSON
RICHARD BUXTON
BRENDA HOGGETT

MICHAEL COLLON, *Secretary*
5 March 1992

Draft

Family Homes and Domestic Violence Bill

ARRANGEMENT OF CLAUSES

DRAFT

OF A

BILL

TO

Amend the law relating to the rights of a husband or wife to occupy the matrimonial home; to make new provision for proceedings relating to the occupation of a dwelling-house which is or has been the home of two or more persons and proceedings relating to the molestation of one person by another; to make new provision for the transfer of tenancies between spouses and persons who have lived together as husband and wife; to apply section 17 of the Married Women's Property Act 1882 to persons who live together as husband and wife; and for connected purposes.

BE IT ENACTED by the Queen's most Excellent Majesty, by and with the advice and consent of the Lords Spiritual and Temporal, and Commons, in this present Parliament assembled, and by the authority of the same, as follows:—

Introductory

Meaning of "cohabitants".

1. For the purposes of this Act—

(a) "cohabitants" are a man and a woman who, although not married to each other, are living with each other as husband and wife; and

(b) "former cohabitants" shall be construed accordingly, but does not include cohabitants who have subsequently married each other.

Associated persons.

2. For the purposes of this Act a person is associated with another person if—

(a) they are or have been married to each other,

(b) they are cohabitants or former cohabitants,

(c) they live or have lived in the same household, otherwise than merely by reason of one of them being the other's employee, tenant, lodger or boarder,

(d) they are relatives,

EXPLANATORY NOTES

Clause 1

1.   This clause defines "cohabitants" and "former cohabitants" for the purposes of this Bill. These terms are discussed in paragraph 3.18 of the report.

Clause 2

1.   This clause defines the range of people who are associated with one another for the purpose of certain orders made under this Bill. Relatives are defined in clause 27(1) below. This clause implements the recommendations in paragraphs 3.26 and 4.9 of the report.

(e) they have at any time agreed to marry each other (whether or not the agreement has been terminated),

(f) they have or have had a sexual relationship with each other (whether or not involving sexual intercourse),

(g) they are the parents of a child or, in relation to any child, are persons who have or have had parental responsibility for that child (whether or not at the same time), or

(h) they are parties to the same family proceedings (other than proceedings under this Act).

Meaning of "relevant child".

3. In this Act a "relevant child", in relation to any proceedings under this Act, means—

(a) any child who is living with or might reasonably be expected to live with either party to the proceedings,

1976 c. 36.
1989 c. 41.

(b) any child in relation to whom an order under the Adoption Act 1976 or the Children Act 1989 is in question in the proceedings, and

(c) any other child whose interests the court considers relevant.

Rights to occupy matrimonial home

Rights concerning matrimonial home where one spouse has no estate, etc.

4.—(1) Where one spouse is entitled to occupy a dwelling-house by virtue of a beneficial estate or interest or contract or by virtue of any enactment giving him the right to remain in occupation, and the other spouse is not so entitled, then, subject to the provisions of this Act, the spouse not so entitled shall have the following rights (in this Act referred to as "matrimonial home rights")—

(a) if in occupation, a right not to be evicted or excluded from the dwelling-house or any part of it by the other spouse except with the leave of the court given by an order under section 7;

(b) if not in occupation, a right with the leave of the court so given to enter into and occupy the dwelling-house.

(2) Where a spouse is entitled under this section to occupy a dwelling-house or any part of a dwelling-house, any payment or tender made or other thing done by that spouse in or towards satisfaction of any liability of the other spouse in respect of rent, mortgage payments or other outgoings affecting the dwelling-house shall, whether or not it is made in pursuance of an order under section 12, be as good as if made or done by the other spouse.

(3) A spouse's occupation by virtue of this section shall—

1976 c. 80.
1977 c. 42.

(a) be treated, for the purposes of the Rent (Agriculture) Act 1976 and the Rent Act 1977 (other than Part V and sections 103 to 106), as occupation by the other spouse as the other spouse's residence, and

1985 c. 68.
1988 c. 50.

(b) if the spouse occupies the dwellinghouse as that spouse's only or principal home, be treated, for the purposes of the Housing Act 1985 and Part I of the Housing Act 1988, as occupation by the other spouse as the other spouse's only or principal home.

EXPLANATORY NOTES

Clause 3

1.   This clause defines a "relevant child" for the purpose of this Bill. This is discussed in paragraph 3.27 of the report.

Clause 4

1.   This clause reproduces (with minor modifications) those subsections of section 1 of the Matrimonial Homes Act 1983 which are specified below. Subsections (2),(3) and (4) of that section which deal with the scope and duration of orders which may be made and the criteria for them are now dealt with separately in clauses 7, 9 and 10. This clause uses the new term "matrimonial home rights" to describe statutory rights of occupation in the home granted under this Bill instead of the term "rights of occupation" used in the 1983 Act.

Subsection(1)
2.   This subsection is derived from section 1(1) of the 1983 Act. It defines the nature and extent of "matrimonial home rights".

Subsection (2)
3.   This subsection is derived from section 1(5) of the 1983 Act. It ensures that a spouse having matrimonial home rights may pay rent, mortgage payments or other outgoings affecting the dwelling-house and that this shall have the same effect as if done by the other spouse.

Subsection (3)
4.   This subsection is derived from section 1(6) of the 1983 Act. It ensures that occupation by a spouse with matrimonial home rights is treated as occupation by the other spouse for the purpose of certain enactments dealing with security of tenure.

        (a) The wording of section 1(6) of the 1983 Act has been amended slightly. Section 1(6) provided that a spouse's occupation be treated as "possession" for the purposes of the Rent (Agriculture) Act 1976 and the Rent Act 1977. However, the protection of these enactments is dependent on the occupation rather than possession of the tenant.

        (b) Similarly, the wording of section 1(6) of the 1983 Act has been amended in order to ensure consistency with the provisions of the Housing Acts. Section 1(6) merely stated that a spouse's occupation by virtue of this section be treated as occupation by the other spouse for the purposes of the Housing Acts. However, in order to obtain protection as a secure tenant or an assured tenant under the Housing Acts, the tenant must occupy the dwelling-house "as his only or principal home".

(4) Where a spouse is entitled under this section to occupy a dwelling-house or any part of a dwelling-house and makes any payment in or towards satisfaction of any liability of the other spouse in respect of mortgage payments affecting the dwelling-house, the person to whom the payment is made may treat it as having been made by that other spouse, but the fact that that person has treated any such payment as having been so made shall not affect any claim of the first-mentioned spouse against the other to an interest in the dwelling-house by virtue of the payment.

(5) Where a spouse is entitled under this section to occupy a dwelling-house or part of a dwelling-house by reason of an interest of the other spouse under a trust, all the provisions of subsections (2) to (4) shall apply in relation to the trustees as they apply in relation to the other spouse.

(6) This section shall not apply to a dwelling-house which has at no time been, and which was at no time intended by the spouses to be, a matrimonial home of the spouses in question.

(7) A spouse's matrimonial home rights shall continue only so long as the marriage subsists and the other spouse is entitled as mentioned in subsection (1) to occupy the dwelling-house, except to the extent that an order under section 7(4) otherwise provides.

(8) It is hereby declared that a spouse who has an equitable interest in a dwelling-house or in its proceeds of sale, not being a spouse in whom there is vested (whether solely or as joint tenant) a legal estate in fee simple or a legal term of years absolute in the dwelling-house, is to be treated for the purpose only of determining whether he has matrimonial home rights as not being entitled to occupy the dwelling-house by virtue of that interest.

Effect of rights of occupation as charge on dwelling house.

5.—(1) Where, at any time during the subsistence of a marriage, one spouse is entitled to occupy a dwelling-house by virtue of a beneficial estate or interest, then the other spouse's matrimonial home rights shall be a charge on that estate or interest, having the like priority as if it were an equitable interest created at whichever is the latest of the following dates—

(a) the date on which the spouse so entitled acquires the estate or interest,

(b) the date of the marriage, and

1967 c. 75.

(c) 1st January 1968 (which is the date of commencement of the Matrimonial Homes Act 1967).

(2) If, at any time when a spouse's matrimonial home rights are a charge on an interest of the other spouse under a trust, there are, apart from either of the spouses, no persons, living or unborn, who are or could become beneficiaries under the trust, then those rights shall be a charge also on the estate or interest of the trustees for the other spouse, having the like priority as if it were an equitable interest created (under powers overriding the trusts) on the date when it arises.

(3) In determining for the purposes of subsection (2) whether there are any persons who are not, but could become, beneficiaries under

Subsection (4)

5.   This subsection reproduces section 1(7) of the 1983 Act without substantive change. It provides that a mortgagee may treat the payment of mortgage instalments by a spouse with matrimonial home rights as having been made by the other spouse. This will not affect the right of the paying spouse to claim the acquisition of an interest in the property by virtue of such payment.

Subsection (5)

6.   This subsection reproduces section 1(8) of the 1983 Act without substantive change. It provides that where a spouse has matrimonial home rights by reason of the other spouse being a beneficiary under a trust, then subsections (2) to (4) above shall apply in relation to the trustees.

Subsection (6)

7.   This subsection is principally derived from section 1(10) of the 1983 Act. It provides that this clause shall only apply in relation to a dwelling-house which, was the matrimonial home or was intended by both spouses to be the matrimonial home.   This implements the recommendation made in paragraph 4.4 of the report.

Subsection (7)

8.   This subsection provides that matrimonial home rights shall continue only as long as both the marriage lasts and the other spouse is entitled to occupy the home in question unless the court makes an order extending the matrimonial home rights under clause 7(4) below.

Subsection (8)

9.   This subsection reproduces section 1(11) of the 1983 Act, without substantive change. It ensures that a spouse who has an equitable as opposed to a legal interest in the home (or in its proceeds of sale) has the same matrimonial home rights as has a spouse who has no interest in the home at all.

Clause 5

1.   This clause reproduces section 2 of the 1983 Act with some minor changes. In particular, the provisions formerly in section 2(5) of the 1983 Act are now included in clause 8 of the Bill and all references in the 1983 Act to "rights of occupation" have been changed to "matrimonial home rights".

Subsections (1)-(3) and (5)-(9)

2.   These subsections reproduce the provisions of section 2(1)-(3), (6) and (8)-(11) respectively of the 1983 Act relating to the effect of matrimonial home rights as a charge on the dwelling-house.

the trust, there shall be disregarded any potential exercise of a general power of appointment exercisable by either or both of the spouses alone (whether or not the exercise of it requires the consent of another person).

(4) Notwithstanding that a spouse's matrimonial home rights are a charge on an estate or interest in the dwelling-house, those rights shall be brought to an end by—

(a) the death of the other spouse, or

(b) the termination (otherwise than by death) of the marriage,

unless the court directs otherwise by an order made under section 7(4) during the subsistence of the marriage.

(5) Where—

(a) a spouse's matrimonial home rights are a charge on an estate or interest in the dwelling-house, and

(b) that estate or interest is surrendered to merge in some other estate or interest expectant on it in such circumstances that, but for the merger, the person taking the estate or interest would be bound by the charge,

the surrender shall have effect subject to the charge and the persons thereafter entitled to the other estate or interest shall, for so long as the estate or interest surrendered would have endured if not so surrendered, be treated for all purposes of this Act as deriving title to the other estate or interest under the other spouse or, as the case may be, under the trustees for the other spouse, by virtue of the surrender.

(6) Where the title to the legal estate by virtue of which a spouse is entitled to occupy a dwelling-house (including any legal estate held by trustees for that spouse) is registered under the Land Registration Act 1925 or any enactment replaced by that Act—

(a) registration of a land charge affecting the dwelling-house by virtue of this Act shall be effected by registering a notice under that Act, and

(b) a spouse's matrimonial home rights shall not be an overriding interest within the meaning of that Act affecting the dwelling-house notwithstanding that the spouse is in actual occupation of the dwelling-house.

(7) A spouse's matrimonial home rights (whether or not constituting a charge) shall not entitle that spouse to lodge a caution under section 54 of the Land Registration Act 1925.

(8) Where—

(a) a spouse's matrimonial home rights are a charge on the estate of the other spouse or of trustees of the other spouse, and

(b) that estate is the subject of a mortgage,

then if, after the date of the creation of the mortgage, the charge is registered under section 2 of the Land Charges Act 1972, the charge shall, for the purposes of section 94 of the Law of Property Act 1925 (which regulates the rights of mortgagees to make further advances ranking in priority to subsequent mortgages), be deemed to be a mortgage subsequent in date to the first-mentioned mortgage.

1925 c. 21.

1972 c. 61
1925 c. 20.

Subsection (4)

3.   This subsection is derived from section 2(4) of the 1983 Act. It provides that matrimonial home rights are brought to an end by the death of the other spouse or the termination of the marriage unless an order is made under section 6(4) below.

(9) It is hereby declared that a charge under subsection (1) or (2) is not registrable under section 2 of the Land Charges Act 1972 or subsection (6) of this section unless it is a charge on a legal estate.

Further provisions relating to matrimonial home rights.

1983 c. 19.

6.—(1) Schedule 1 (which re-enacts with consequential amendments and minor modifications provisions of the Matrimonial Homes Act 1983) shall have effect.

Occupation orders

Occupation orders where applicant has estate or interest etc.

7.—(1) Where—

  (a) a person ("the person entitled")—

    (i) is entitled to occupy a dwelling-house by virtue of a beneficial estate or interest or contract or by virtue of any enactment giving him the right to remain in occupation, or

    (ii) has matrimonial home rights in relation to a dwelling-house, and

  (b) the dwelling-house—

    (i) is or at any time has been the home of the person entitled and of another person with whom he is associated, or

    (ii) was at any time intended by the person entitled and any such other person to be their home,

the person entitled may apply to the court for an order containing any of the provisions specified in subsections (2), (3) and (4).

(2) An order under this section may—

  (a) enforce the applicant's entitlement to remain in occupation as against the other person ("the respondent"),

  (b) require the respondent to permit the applicant to enter and remain in the dwelling-house or part of the dwelling-house,

  (c) regulate the occupation of the dwelling-house by either or both parties,

  (d) where the respondent is entitled as mentioned in subsection (1)(a)(i), prohibit, suspend or restrict the exercise by him of his right to occupy the dwelling-house,

  (e) where the respondent has matrimonial home rights in relation to the dwelling-house and the applicant is the other spouse, restrict or terminate those rights,

  (f) require the respondent to leave the dwelling-house or part of the dwelling-house, or

  (g) exclude the respondent from a defined area in which the dwelling-house is included.

(3) An order under this section may declare that the applicant is entitled as mentioned in subsection (1)(a)(i) or has matrimonial home rights.

(4) Where the applicant has matrimonial home rights and the respondent is the other spouse, an order under this section may

EXPLANATORY NOTES

Clause 6

This clause gives effect to Schedule 1 of the Bill.

Clause 7

1.   This clause deals with the power of the court to make occupation orders where the applicant is entitled to occupy the dwelling-house either by virtue of the general law or by virtue of matrimonial home rights under clause 4.

Subsection (1)
2.   This subsection provides that any person so entitled may apply for an occupation order against anyone with whom he is associated as defined in clause 2 above, provided that the dwelling-house in question is, was or was intended by both parties to be their common home. This implements the recommendations made in paragraphs 4.4 and 4.9 of the report.

Subsections (2), (5) and (6)
3.   Subsection (2) lists the regulatory orders which may be included in an order made under this clause. This implements part of the recommendation in paragraph 4.2 of the report. The factors to which the court is to have regard in making regulatory orders are set out in subsection (5), but these are subject to the "balance of harm" test in subsection (6). This imposes an overriding requirement for the court to make an order if it appears that the applicant or a child is likely to suffer significant harm if an order is not made greater than the respondent or a child is likely to suffer if the order is made. "Harm" is defined in clause 27(1) below. This implements the recommendations made in paragraph 4.33 of the report.

Subsection (3)
4.   This subsection gives the court power to declare that an applicant is entitled to occupy a dwelling house or has matrimonial home rights. It implements the recommendation made in paragraph 4.2 of the report.

Subsections (4) and (7)
5.   These subsections enable the court to provide for matrimonial home rights to continue after the death of the other spouse or the termination of the marriage where it considers that it in all the circumstances it is just and reasonable to do so. This implements the recommendation made in paragraph 4.3 of the report.

provide that those rights shall not be brought to an end by—

(a) the death of the other spouse, or

(b) the termination (otherwise than by death) of the marriage.

(5) In deciding whether to exercise its powers under subsection (2) and, if so, in what manner, the court shall have regard to all the circumstances including—

(a) the respective housing needs and resources of the parties and of any relevant child,

(b) the respective financial resources of the parties,

(c) the likely effect of any order, or of any decision by the court not to exercise its powers under subsection (2), on the health, safety or well-being of the parties and of any relevant child,

but subject to subsection (6).

(6) If it appears to the court that the applicant or any relevant child is likely to suffer significant harm if an order under this section containing one or more of the provisions mentioned in subsection (2) is not made, the court shall make the order unless it appears to the court that—

(a) the respondent or any relevant child is likely to suffer significant harm if the order is made, and

(b) the harm likely to be suffered by the respondent or child in that event is greater than the harm likely to be suffered by the applicant or child if the order is not made.

(7) The court may exercise its powers under subsection (4) in any case where it considers that in all the circumstances it is just and reasonable to do so.

(8) An order under this section—

(a) may not be made after the death of either of the parties mentioned in subsection (1), and

(b) except in the case of an order made by virtue of subsection (4)(a), shall cease to have effect on the death of either party.

(9) An order under this section—

(a) may, in so far as it has continuing effect, be made for a specified period, until the occurrence of a specified event or until further order, and

(b) may be varied or revoked.

Effect of order under section 7 where rights are charge on dwelling-house.

8.—(1) Where a spouse's matrimonial home rights are a charge on the estate or interest of the other spouse or of trustees for the other spouse—

(a) any order under section 7 against the other spouse shall, except so far as a contrary intention appears, have the like effect against persons deriving title under the other spouse or under the trustees and affected by the charge, and

(b) subsections (1), (2), (3) and (9) of that section and subsections (2) to (5) of section 4 shall apply in relation to any person deriving title under the other spouse or under the trustees and affected by the charge as they apply in relation to the

EXPLANATORY NOTES

Subsection (8)

6.   This subsection makes it clear that an order could not be made after the death of either party, nor continue to have effect after the death of the respondent unless an order extending matrimonial home rights has been made under subsection (4).

Subsection (9)

7.   This subsection deals with the duration of an order under clause 7 and implements the recommendation in paragraph 4.36 of the report.

Clause 8

1.   This clause is derived from section 2(5) of the Matrimonial Homes Act 1983. It deals with the effect of an order under clause 7 where one spouse's matrimonial home rights are a charge on the estate or interest of the other spouse or of the trustees for the other spouse and a person has derived title under the other spouse or under the trustees.

Subsection (1)

2.   Paragraph (a) provides that such persons are affected by the charge as it applies in relation to the other spouse. Paragraph (b) applies subsections (1), (2),(3) and (9) of clause 7 and subsections (2) to (5) of clause 4 to such persons.

other spouse.

(2) The court may make an order under section 7 by virtue of this section where it considers that in all the circumstances it is just and reasonable to do so.

Occupation orders where applicant has no existing right to occupy.

9.—(1) Where—

(a) one cohabitant, former cohabitant or former spouse is entitled to occupy a dwelling-house which—

(i) in the case of cohabitants or former cohabitants, is the home in which they live together as husband and wife or a home in which they at any time so lived together or intended so to live together, or

(ii) in the case of former spouses, was at any time their matrimonial home or was at any time intended by them to be their matrimonial home,

by virtue of a beneficial estate or interest or contract or by virtue of any enactment giving him the right to remain in occupation, and

(b) the other cohabitant, former cohabitant or former spouse is not so entitled,

the cohabitant, former cohabitant or former spouse not so entitled may apply to the court for an order under this section against the other cohabitant, former cohabitant or former spouse ("the respondent").

(2) Every order under this section must contain the following provision—

(a) if the applicant is in occupation, provision giving the applicant the right not to be evicted or excluded from the dwelling-house or any part of it by the respondent for the period specified in the order and prohibiting the respondent from evicting or excluding the applicant during that period, or

(b) if the applicant is not in occupation, provision giving the applicant the right to enter into and occupy the dwelling-house for the period specified in the order and requiring the respondent to permit the exercise of that right.

(3) An order under this section may in addition contain any of the provisions mentioned in section 7(2)(c), (d), (f) and (g).

(4) In deciding whether to exercise its powers to make an order under this section containing such provision as is mentioned in subsection (2), and if so in what manner, the court shall have regard to all the circumstances including the matters mentioned in section 7(5)(a), (b) and (c) and the following further matters—

(a) where the parties are cohabitants or former cohabitants, the nature of their relationship, the length of time during which they have lived with each other as husband and wife and whether there are or have been any children who are children of both parties or for whom both parties have or have had parental responsibility,

Subsection (2)

3.   This subsection prescribes a broad criterion for making an order under this clause.

Clause 9

1.   This clause deals with the power of the court to make occupation orders when the applicant is not entitled to occupy the dwelling-house but the respondent is so entitled. Such applications may only be made between cohabitants, former cohabitants and former spouses and have more restrictive criteria and effects than have orders in favour of applicants who are entitled to occupy. This implements the recommendation made in paragraph 4.9(b) of the report.

Subsection (1)

2.   This subsection provides that such an applicant may apply for an order under this clause in relation to a dwelling-house which, in the case of cohabitants or former cohabitants, is the home in which they lived, are living or both intended to live together as husband and wife or, in the case of former spouses was the matrimonial home or was intended by both to be the matrimonial home. This implements the recommendations in paragraphs 4.4 and 4.9 of the report.

Subsection (2)

3.   This subsection provides that every order made under this clause confers certain occupation rights upon the applicant for the duration of the order. The criteria to be applied by the court are set out in sub-section (4) below. This implements the first recommendation in paragraph 4.18 of the report.

Subsection (3)

4.   This subsection provides that in addition to granting an occupation rights order under subsection (2), an order made under this clause may contain any of the regulatory orders listed in clause 7(2)(c), (d), (f) and (g).

Subsection (4)

5.   This subsection sets out the criteria to which the court is to have regard in exercising its power to grant occupation rights under subsection (2). It requires the court to consider the criteria prescribed in clause 7(5) above in relation to regulatory orders, together with three qualifying criteria specific to non-entitled applicants which take into account the nature and duration of the parties' relationship, how recently they parted and the existence of any proceedings pending between them for financial provision or relating to the legal or beneficial ownership of the dwelling house. It implements the recommendation made in paragraph 4.13 and part of the second recommendation in paragraph 4.18 of the report.

> (b) where the parties are former cohabitants or former spouses, the length of time that has elapsed since the parties ceased to live with each other and, in the case of former spouses, the length of time that has elapsed since the marriage was dissolved or annulled, and

> (c) the existence of any pending proceedings between the parties—

1973 c. 18.

>> (i) for an order under section 24 of the Matrimonial Causes Act 1973,

1989 c. 41.

>> (ii) for an order under paragraph 1(2)(d) or (e) of Schedule 1 to the Children Act 1989, or

>> (ii) relating to the legal or beneficial ownership of the dwelling-house.

(5) In deciding whether to exercise its powers under subsection (3) and, if so, in what manner, the court shall have regard to all the circumstances including the matters mentioned in subsection (5)(a), (b) and (c) of section 7, but subject to subsection (6) of this section.

(6) Where the court decides to make an order under this section and it appears to the court that, if the order does not include one or more of the additional provisions mentioned in section 7(2)(c), (d), (f) and (g) (a "restriction or exclusion provision"), the applicant or any relevant child is likely to suffer significant harm, the court shall include the restriction or exclusion provision in the order unless it appears to the court that—

> (a) the respondent or any relevant child is likely to suffer significant harm if the restriction or exclusion provision is included in the order, and

> (b) the harm likely to be suffered by the respondent or child in that event is greater than the harm likely to be suffered by the applicant or child if the restriction or exclusion provision is not included.

(7) An order under this section—

> (a) may not be made after the death of either of the parties mentioned in subsection (1), and

> (b) shall cease to have effect on the death of either party.

(8) An order under this section shall be limited so as to have effect for a specified period not exceeding six months, but—

> (a) may be extended (on one or more occasions) for a further specified period not exceeding six months, and

> (b) may be varied or revoked at any time.

(9) A person who has an equitable interest in the dwelling-house or in the proceeds of sale of the dwelling-house but in whom there is not vested (whether solely or as joint tenant) a legal estate in fee simple or a legal term of years absolute in the dwelling-house is to be treated only for the purpose of determining whether he is eligible to apply under subsection (1) as not being so entitled, but this subsection does not prejudice any right of such a person to apply for an order under section 7.

EXPLANATORY NOTES

Subsections (5) and (6)

6.   These subsections deal with the criteria for the grant of the regulatory orders listed in clause 7(2)(c), (d), (f) and (g) above to non-entitled applicants who have been granted occupation rights. Subsection (5) directs the court to apply the criteria prescribed in relation to regulatory orders in clause 7(5)(a), (b) and (c) above, subject to the application of the balance of harm test set out in subsection (6) under which the court is directed to make a regulatory order if it appears that the applicant or a child is likely to suffer significant harm if a regulatory order is not made greater than the respondent or a child is likely to suffer if a regulatory order is made.   "Harm" is defined in clause 27(1) below.   This implements the recommendation in paragraph 4.33 and part of the second recommendation made in paragraph 4.18 of the report.

Subsection (7)

7.   This subsection makes it clear that an order under this section could not be made, nor continue to have effect, after the death of either party.

Subsection (8)

8.   This subsection provides that orders in favour of non-entitled applicants should be of limited duration. It implements the recommendation in paragraph 4.37 of the report.

Subsection (9)

10.   This subsection ensures that an applicant who has only an equitable as opposed to a legal interest in the dwelling-house (or in its proceeds of sale) may be protected. This is done by treating such an applicant as non-entitled for the purposes of determining whether he is eligible to apply under this clause.

(10) If a person is given the right mentioned in subsection (2)(a) or (b) by virtue of an order under this section, then, so long as the order remains in force, subsections (2) to (5) of section 4 shall apply in relation to that person—

(a) as if he were a spouse entitled to occupy the dwelling-house by virtue of that section, and

(b) as if the respondent were the other spouse.

Occupation orders where neither party entitled to occupy.

10.—(1) Where one spouse, former spouse, cohabitant or former cohabitant and the other spouse, former spouse, cohabitant or former cohabitant occupy a dwelling-house which—

(a) in the case of cohabitants or former cohabitants, is the home in which they live or lived together as husband and wife, or

(b) in the case of spouses or former spouses, is or was the matrimonial home,

but neither of them is entitled to remain in occupation by virtue of a beneficial estate or interest or by virtue of any enactment giving him the right to remain in occupation, either of the parties may apply to the court for an order against the other under this section.

(2) An order under this section may make any of the provisions mentioned in section 7(2)(b), (c), (f) and (g).

(3) Subsections (5) and (6) of section 7 shall apply to the exercise by the court of its powers under this section as it applies to the exercise by the court of its powers under subsection (2) of that section.

(4) An order under this section may be varied or revoked.

Provisions supplementary to ss. 7, 9 and 10.

11.—(1) In this Act an "occupation order" means an order under section 7, 9 or 10.

(2) An application for an occupation order may be made in other family proceedings or without any other family proceedings being instituted.

(3) If—

(a) an application for an occupation order is made under section 7, 9 or 10, and

(b) the court considers that it has no power to make the order under the section concerned, but that it has power to make an order under one of the other sections,

the court may make an order under that other section.

(4) The fact that a person has applied for an occupation order under section 9 or 10, or that such an order has been made, shall not affect the right of any person to claim a legal or equitable interest in any property in any subsequent proceedings (including subsequent proceedings under this Act), unless in the proceedings under section 9 or 10 the court has by order declared the respective rights of the parties in the property concerned.

EXPLANATORY NOTES

Subsection (10)

11.   This subsection gives a person with the benefit of an occupation rights order the same protection under subsections (2) to (5) of section 4 as a spouse with matrimonial home rights. This includes treating occupation by that person as occupation by the respondent for the purpose of certain statutory enactments and allowing a mortgagee to treat the payment of mortgage instalments by that person as though made by the respondent.

Clause 10

Subsection (1)

1.   This subsection gives the court power to make occupation orders between spouses, former spouses, cohabitants and former cohabitants where neither party is entitled to occupy the dwelling-house. It reproduces the effect of the Domestic Violence and Matrimonial Proceedings Act 1976 in this respect. It might be used, for example, where neither party wished to assert a right to occupy or where they could not prove one. The clause implements the recommendations in paragraphs 4.4 and 4.9 of the report and is discussed in paragraph 4.8.

Subsection (2)

2.   This subsection enables the court to make such of the regulatory orders listed in clause 7(2) as might be relevant between two non-entitled parties: namely, to regulate the occupation of the dwelling-house; to require the respondent to allow the applicant to enter and remain in the dwelling-house; to require the respondent to leave the dwelling-house or part thereof; and/or to exclude the respondent from a defined area around the dwelling-house.

Subsection (3)

3.   This subsection provides that in making orders under this clause, the court shall apply the same criteria as it applies in exercising its powers to make regulatory orders under clause 7(5) and (6).

Clause 11

1.   This clause contains provisions supplementary to clauses 7, 9 and 10 which govern the powers of the court to grant occupation orders.

Subsection (2)

2.   This subsection deals with the court's jurisdiction to hear applications for occupation orders and implements the recommendation in paragraph 5.3 of the report.

Subsection (3)

3.   This subsection permits the court on hearing an application for an occupation order made under one of these three clauses, to make an order under either of the other two clauses if it considers that this would be appropriate.   The purpose of this is to ensure that the court is not required to dismiss an application for an occupation order simply because the application has been made under the wrong clause, either in error or because it transpires during the hearing that an apparently non-entitled party is in fact entitled, or vice versa.

Additional
provisions that
may be included
in certain
occupation
orders.

12.—(1) The court may on making an occupation order under section 7 or 9 or at any time thereafter—

(a) impose on either party obligations as to the repair and mainte- nance of the dwelling-house or as to the discharge of rent, mortgage payments or other outgoings affecting the dwelling- house,

(b) order a party occupying the dwelling-house or any part of it (including a party who is entitled to do so by virtue of a beneficial estate or interest or by virtue of any enactment giving him the right to remain in occupation) to make periodical payments to the other party in respect of the accommodation, where the other party would (but for the order) be entitled to occupy the dwelling-house by virtue of a beneficial estate or interest or by virtue of any such enactment, and

(c) grant either party possession or use of furniture or other contents of the dwelling-house.

(2) In deciding whether and, if so, how to exercise its powers under this section, the court shall have regard to all the circumstances of the case including—

(a) the financial resources of the parties, and

(b) the financial obligations which they have, or are likely to have in the foreseeable future, including financial obligations to each other or to any relevant child.

(3) An order under this section shall cease to have effect when the occupation order to which it relates ceases to have effect.

Non-molestation orders

Non-molestation
orders.

13.—(1) In this Act a "non-molestation order" means an order containing either or both of the following provisions—

(a) provision prohibiting a person ("the respondent") from molesting another person who is associated with the respon- dent, and

(b) provision prohibiting the respondent from molesting a relevant child.

(2) The court may make a non-molestation order—

(a) if an application for the order has been made by a person who is associated with the respondent, or

(b) if in any family proceedings to which the respondent is a party the court considers that the order should be made for the benefit of any other party to the proceedings or any relevant child even though no such application has been made.

(3) In deciding whether to exercise its powers under this section and, if so, in what manner, the court shall have regard to all the circumstances including the need to secure the health, safety and well-being—

(a) of the applicant or, in a case falling within subsection (2)(b), the person for whose benefit the order would be made, and

Subsection (4)

4.   This subsection ensures that neither an application nor an order under a particular clause will prevent either party from subsequently claiming an interest in the property unless the court has adjudicated upon the issue.

Clause 12

Subsection (1)

1.   This subsection provides for the court when granting an occupation order under clauses 7 or 9 to make ancillary orders relating to the maintenance and repair of the property and the discharge of rent, mortgage payments or other outgoings by either party. The court can also order the occupying party to pay rent to an entitled respondent who has been ousted, and make orders relating to the use of furniture and contents. This implements the recommendation in paragraph 4.42 of the report.

Subsection (2)

2.   This subsection prescribes the criteria for the grant of ancillary orders.

Subsection (3)

3.   This subsection provides that ancillary orders shall lapse automatically when the occupation order ceases to have effect.

Clause 13

1.   This clause deals with the power of the court, either of its own motion or upon application, to grant non-molestation orders. This implements the recommendation in paragraph 3.1 of the report.

Subsection (1)

2.   This subsection defines the people whom a respondent may be prohibited from molesting. These are people who are associated with the respondent within the meaning of clause 2 above and any relevant children.

Subsection (2)

3.   This subsection gives the court power to make a non-molestation order either upon application or of its own motion in family proceedings. It implements the recommendation in paragraph 5.3 in the report.

Subsection (3)

4.   This subsection prescribes a broad criterion for the grant of non-molestation orders and implements the recommendation in paragraph 3.7 of the report.

(b) of any relevant child.

(4) A non-molestation order may be expressed so as to refer to molestation in general, to particular acts of molestation, or to both.

(5) A non-molestation order may be made for a specified period or until further order and may be varied or revoked.

Further provisions relating to occupation orders and non-molestation orders

Ex parte orders.

14.—(1) The court may, in any case where it considers that it is just and convenient to do so, make an occupation order or a non-molestation order even though the respondent has not been given such notice of the proceedings as may be prescribed by rules of court.

(2) In determining whether to exercise its powers under subsection (1) the court shall have regard to all the circumstances including—

  (a) any risk of significant harm to the applicant or a relevant child if the order is not made immediately,

  (b) whether it is likely that the applicant will be deterred or prevented from pursuing the application if an order is not made immediately, and

  (c) whether there is reason to believe that the respondent is aware of the proceedings but is deliberately evading service and that the applicant or a relevant child will be seriously prejudiced by the delay involved—

    (i) where the court is a magistrates' court, in effecting service of proceedings, or

    (ii) in any other case, in effecting substituted service.

Arrest for breach of order.

15.—(1) In this section "a relevant order" means an occupation order or a non-molestation order.

(2) Where—

  (a) the court makes a relevant order, and

  (b) it appears to the court that the respondent has used or threatened violence against the applicant or a relevant child,

the court shall attach a power of arrest to specified provisions of the order unless the court is satisfied that in all the circumstances of the case the applicant or child will be adequately protected without such a power of arrest.

(3) Subsection (2) does not apply in any case where the relevant order is made by virtue of section 14(1), but in such a case the court may attach a power of arrest to specified provisions of the order if it appears to the court—

  (a) that the respondent has used or threatened violence against the applicant or a relevant child, and

  (b) that there is a risk of significant harm to the applicant or child if the power of arrest is not attached to those provisions immediately.

(4) If, by virtue of subsection (2) or (3), a power of arrest is attached to specified provisions of an order, a constable may arrest

EXPLANATORY NOTES

Subsection (4)

5.　　This subsection implements the recommendation in paragraph 3.2 of the report.

Subsection (5)

6.　　This subsection implements the recommendation in paragraph 3.28 of the report.

Clause 14

1.　　This clause deals with the power of the court to make ex parte orders. It implements the recommendation in paragraph 5.10 of the report.

Subsection (1)

2.　　This subsection empowers the court to make occupation or non-molestation orders ex parte or on short notice.

Subsection (2)

3.　　This subsection prescribes the matters to be considered by the court when hearing an application for an ex parte order.

Clause 15

1.　　This clause deals with the court's powers to arrest for breach of and to attach a power of arrest to an occupation or non-molestation order. It extends and brings into line in all courts the enforcement procedures formerly found in section 18 of the Domestic Proceedings and Magistrates' Courts Act 1976 and section 2 of the Domestic Violence and Matrimonial Proceedings Act 1976.

Subsection (2)

2.　　This subsection requires the court to attach a power of arrest to specified provisions of an occupation or non-molestation order if the respondent has used or threatened violence against the applicant or a child concerned, unless this is unnecessary for their protection. This implements the recommendation in paragraph 5.13 of the report.

Subsection (3)

3.　　This subsection provides that a power of arrest may be attached to an ex parte order where there has been actual or threatened violence and additionally, there is a risk of significant harm (as defined in clause 27(1)) to the applicant or a child if the power of arrest is not attached immediately. This implements the recommendation in paragraph 5.14 of the report.

Subsection (4)

4.　　This subsection provides that once a power of arrest has been attached to an order, a constable may arrest the respondent without a warrant if he has reasonable cause to believe that there has been a breach of the provisions to which the power of arrest was attached.

without warrant a person whom he has reasonable cause for suspecting to be in breach of any such provision.

(5) Where a power of arrest is attached under subsection (2) or (3) to specified provisions of the order and the respondent is arrested under subsection (4)—

    (a) he shall be brought before the relevant judicial authority within the period of 24 hours beginning at the time of his arrest, and

    (b) the relevant judicial authority before whom he is brought may remand him.

In reckoning for the purposes of this subsection any period of 24 hours, no account shall be taken of Christmas Day, Good Friday or any Sunday.

(6) Where the court has made a relevant order but has not attached a power of arrest under subsection (2) or (3) to any provisions of the order or has attached that power only to certain provisions of the order, then, if at any time the applicant considers that the respondent has failed to comply with the order, he may apply to the relevant judicial authority for the issue of a warrant for the arrest of the respondent.

(7) The relevant judicial authority shall not issue a warrant on an application under subsection (6) unless—

    (a) the application is substantiated on oath, and

    (b) the relevant judicial authority has reasonable grounds for believing that the respondent has failed to comply with the order.

(8) The court before whom any person is brought by virtue of a warrant issued under subsection (7) may remand him.

(9) Schedule 2 (which makes provision corresponding to that applying in magistrates' courts in civil cases under sections 128 and 129 of the Magistrates' Courts Act 1980) shall have effect in relation to the powers of the High Court and a county court to remand a person by virtue of this section.

1980 c. 43.

(10) In this section "the relevant judicial authority" means—

    (a) where the order was made by the High Court, a judge of that court,

    (b) where the order was made by a county court, a judge or district judge of that or any other county court, and

    (c) where the order was made by a magistrates' court, any justice of the peace.

Remand for medical examination and report.

16.—(1) Any power to remand a person under section 15(5)(b) or (8) may be exercised for the purpose of enabling a medical examination and report to be made, but if such a power is so exercised the adjournment shall not be for more than 4 weeks at a time unless the relevant judicial authority remands the accused in custody and, where the relevant judicial authority so remands him, the adjournment shall not be for more than 3 weeks at a time.

Subsections (5) and (9)

5.　　　Subsection (5) creates a new power of remand in the High Court and county courts. It implements the recommendation in paragraph 5.16 of the report. This subsection also re-enacts the existing law by providing that a respondent who is arrested under a power of arrest must be brought before a judge or justice of the peace within 24 hours. Subsection (9) gives effect to Schedule 2 which creates a remand scheme for the High Court and county courts similar to that already operating in the magistrates' courts by virtue of sections 128 and 129 of the Magistrates' Courts Act 1980.

Subsection (6)

6.　　　This subsection empowers any court, on application, to issue a warrant for the respondent's arrest for breach of any provisions of an occupation or non-molestation order to which no power of arrest has been attached. This replaces the existing power in section 18(4) of the Domestic Proceedings and Magistrates' Courts Act 1978 and extends it to the High Court and county courts, implementing the recommendation in paragraph 5.15 of the report.

Subsection (7)

7.　　　This subsection provides that an arrest warrant should not be issued under subsection (6) unless certain conditions are satisfied. It is derived from section 18(4) of the Domestic Proceedings and Magistrates' Courts Act 1978 which is repealed by Schedule 4 below.

Subsection (8)

8.　　　This subsection enables the court to remand a respondent arrested pursuant to an arrest warrant.

Subsection (10)

9.　　　This subsection ensures that orders made by a particular court should be enforced at the same level, so that, for example, a person arrested pursuant to a power of arrest attached to an order made in a county court will be brought before and dealt with by a judge or district judge of that or another county court. He cannot be dealt with in the magistrates' court or the High Court.

Clause 16

1.　　　This clause gives the court new powers to remand the respondent for medical examination and reports. It implements the recommendations made in paragraph 5.17 of the report.

Subsection (1)

2.　　　This subsection provides that a remand may be made under section 15 above for medical examination and reports and prescribes time limits for remands under this clause.

1983 c. 20.

(2) The relevant judicial authority shall have the like power to make an order under section 35 of the Mental Health Act 1983 (remand for report on accused's mental condition) where there is reason to suspect that a person who has been arrested under section 15(4) or under a warrant issued under section 15(7) is suffering from mental illness or severe mental impairment as the Crown Court has under section 35 of that Act in the case of an accused person within the meaning of that section.

(3) In this section "the relevant judicial authority" has the same meaning as in section 15.

Power of police to apply for orders.

17.—(1) This section applies where a constable—

(a) has attended at or following an alleged incident of molestation, violence or threatened violence between associated persons, and

(b) has reasonable cause to believe that a person ("the aggrieved person") has been subjected to molestation, violence or threatened violence (whether in the course of that incident or otherwise), and

(c) having ascertained so far as practicable the wishes of the aggrieved person, considers that it is appropriate for the constable to apply for an occupation order or a non-molestation order.

(2) Where this section applies, the constable concerned or any constable who is a member of the same police force as that constable may apply to the court on behalf of the aggrieved person for any occupation order or non-molestation order for which the aggrieved person could himself have applied.

(3) Where an application for a non-molestation order or an occupation order is made by virtue of subsection (2)—

(a) the court shall, in determining whether, and if so how, to exercise its powers under section 7, 9, 10 or 13, have regard to any wishes expressed by the aggrieved person (as well as to the other matters to which it is obliged under this Act to have regard), and

(b) references in this Act to the applicant for a non-molestation order or an occupation order shall have effect as references to the aggrieved person.

Interim care orders and emergency protection orders under Children Act 1989

Amendments of Children Act 1989.

18. Schedule 3 (which makes amendments of the provisions of the Children Act 1989 relating to interim care orders and emergency protection orders) shall have effect.

1989 c. 41.

EXPLANATORY NOTES

Subsection (2)
3.   This subsection enables the court to make an order under section 35 of the Mental Health Act 1983 remanding for medical reports a person arrested under a power of arrest or an arrest warrant where there is reason to suspect he is suffering from mental illness or severe mental impairment.

Clause 17

1.   This clause gives the police power to apply for an occupation or non-molestation order on behalf of a victim of domestic violence, molestation or other abuse.   It implements the recommendations in paragraphs 5.20 and 5.23 of the report.

Subsection (1)
2.   This subsection provides that to make such an application, a constable must have attended at or following an alleged incident of molestation, violence or threatened violence between persons who are associated as defined in clause 2; must have reasonable cause to believe that the victim has been subjected to such molestation, violence or threatened violence; and must consider it appropriate to apply for the order having at least attempted to ascertain the wishes of the victim.   This last requirement is intended to give the victim as much control over any proceedings as possible without the burden of the final decision.

Subsection (2)
3.   This subsection makes it clear that a constable can apply for any order on behalf of the victim for which the victim could himself have applied.   The application need not be made by the particular constable who attended at or following the incident of domestic violence concerned, but may be made by any member of the same police force.

Subsection (3)
4.   This subsection requires the court to have regard to the victim's wishes when considering whether to make an order. It also provides, when an application is made by the police, for references in the Bill to the applicant to be read as references to the victim.

Clause 18

1.   This clause gives effect to Schedule 3, which makes amendments to the provisions of the Children Act 1989 relating to interim care orders and emergency protection orders. This implements the recommendation in paragraph 6.17 of the report.

Transfer of tenancies

Transfer of
certain tenancies
on divorce etc.
or on separation
of cohabitants.

19. Schedule 4 shall have effect.

Dwelling-house subject to mortgage

20.—(1) In determining for the purposes of the preceding provisions of this Act (including Schedules 1 and 4) whether a person is entitled to occupy a dwelling-house by virtue of an estate or interest, there shall be disregarded any right to possession of the dwelling-house conferred on a mortgagee of the dwelling-house under or by virtue of his mortgage, whether the mortgagee is in possession or not.

(2) Where a person ("the person entitled") is entitled as mentioned in subsection (1), his spouse, former spouse, cohabitant or former cohabitant shall not by virtue of—

(a) any matrimonial home rights conferred by section 4, or

(b) any rights conferred by an order under section 9,

have any larger right against the mortgagee to occupy the dwelling-house than the person entitled has by virtue of his estate or interest and of any contract with the mortgagee, unless in the case of matrimonial home rights those rights are under section 5 a charge, affecting the mortgagee, on the estate or interest mortgaged.

(3) Where a mortgagee of land which consists of or includes a dwelling-house brings an action in any court for the enforcement of his security, a spouse, former spouse, cohabitant or former cohabitant who is not a party to the action and who is enabled by subsection (2) or (5) of section 4 (or by those subsections as applied by section 9(10)) to meet the mortgagor's liabilities under the mortgage, on applying to the court at any time before the action is finally disposed of in that court, shall be entitled to be made a party to the action if the court—

(a) does not see special reason against it, and

(b) is satisfied that the applicant may be expected to make such payments or do such other things in or towards satisfaction of the mortgagor's liabilities or obligations as might affect the outcome of the proceedings or that the expectation of it should be considered under section 36 of the Administration of Justice Act 1970.

(4) Where a mortgagee of land which consists of or substantially consists of a dwelling-house brings an action for the enforcement of his security, and at the relevant time there is—

(a) in the case of unregistered land, a land charge of Class F registered against the person who is the estate owner at the relevant time or any person who, where the estate owner is a trustee, preceded him as trustee during the subsistence of the mortgage, or

(b) in the case of registered land, a subsisting registration of a notice under section 5(6) of this Act or section 2(8) of the

EXPLANATORY NOTES

Clause 19

1.　　This clause gives effect to Schedule 4 which deals with the transfer of certain tenancies on divorce or on the separation of cohabitants. This implements the recommendation in paragraph 6.6 of the report.

Clause 20

1.　　This clause is derived from section 8 of the Matrimonial Homes Act 1983, which is substantially reproduced. Its provisions deal principally with the effect of matrimonial home rights and occupation rights orders on mortgages and the registration of charges.

Subsections (1), (2) and (3)
2.　　These subsections reproduce section 8(1) and (2) of the 1983 Act and extend their provisions to cohabitants and former cohabitants.

Subsection (4),(5) and (6)
4.　　These subsections reproduce subsections 8(3), (4) and (5) of the 1983 Act respectively, with consequential amendments only.

Matrimonial Homes Act 1983 or a notice or caution under section 2(7) of the Matrimonial Homes Act 1967,

notice of the action shall be served by the mortgagee on the person on whose behalf the land charge is registered or the notice or caution entered, if that person is not a party to the action.

(5) For the purposes of subsection (4), if there has been issued a certificate of the result of an official search made on behalf of the mortgagee which would disclose any land charge of Class F, notice or caution within subsection (4)(a) or (b), and the action is commenced within the priority period, the relevant time is the date of that certificate; and in any other case the relevant time means the time when the action is commenced.

(6) In subsection (5), "priority period" means, for both registered and unregistered land, the period for which, in accordance with section 11(5) and (6) of the Land Charges Act 1972, a certificate on an official search operates in favour of a purchaser.

Property disputes between cohabitants

21.—(1) Section 17 of the Married Women's Property Act 1882 ("the 1882 Act") and section 7 of the Matrimonial Causes (Property and Maintenance) Act 1958 ("the 1958 Act") (which confer power on a judge of the High Court or a county court to settle disputes between husband and wife about property) shall apply, as if the parties were married, to any question arising between cohabitants or former cohabitants as to the title to or possession of property, but subject to subsection (2).

(2) Where the parties are former cohabitants, any application made by virtue of this section under section 17 of the 1882 Act, as originally enacted or as extended by section 7 of the 1958 Act, must be made within the period of three years beginning with the day on which they ceased to live together as husband and wife.

Jurisdiction and procedure etc.

22.—(1) For the purposes of this Act "the court" means the High Court, a county court or a magistrates' court.

(2) Subsection (1) is subject to the provision made by or under the following provisions of this section, to section 23 and to any express provision as to the jurisdiction of any court made by any other provision of this Act.

(3) The Lord Chancellor may by order specify proceedings under this Act which may only be commenced in—

(a) a specified level of court,

(b) a court which falls within a specified class of court, or

(c) a particular court determined in accordance with, or specified in, the order.

(4) The Lord Chancellor may by order specify circumstances in which specified proceedings under this Act may only be commenced in—

EXPLANATORY NOTES

Clause 21

1.   This clause allows cohabitants and former cohabitants to use the summary procedure under section 17 of the Married Women's Property Act 1882 and section 7 of the Matrimonial Causes (Property and Maintenance) Act 1958 to resolve property disputes.   This was formerly available only to married or engaged couples.   It implements the recommendation in paragraph 6.14 of the report.

Subsection (1)
2.   This subsection gives the High Court and county court jurisdiction to settle disputes as to title to or possession of property between cohabitants under the above procedure.

Subsection (2)
3.   This subsection provides that an application by a former cohabitant must be made within three years from the day the parties ceased to live together as husband and wife.

Clause 22

1.   This clause deals with the jurisdiction of the courts under this Bill.

Subsection (1)
2.   This subsection provides for a unified jurisdiction between the High Court, county courts and magistrates' courts, except as otherwise provided in subsection (2).

Subsections (3) - (8)
3.   These subsections govern the making of orders in relation to the commencement and transfer of proceedings under this Bill.

(a) a specified level of court,

(b) a court which falls within a specified class of court, or

(c) a particular court determined in accordance with, or specified in, the order.

(5) The Lord Chancellor may by order provide that in specified circumstances the whole, or any specified part of any specified proceedings under this Act shall be transferred to—

(a) a specified level of court,

(b) a court which falls within a specified class of court, or

(c) a particular court determined in accordance with, or specified in, the order.

(6) Any order under subsection (5) may provide for the transfer to be made at any stage, or specified stage, of the proceedings and whether or not the proceedings, or any part of them, have already been transferred.

1984 c.42

(7) An order under subsection (5) above may make such provision as the Lord Chancellor thinks appropriate for excluding specified proceedings from the operation of section 38 or 39 of the Matrimonial and Family Proceedings Act 1984 (transfer of family proceedings) or any other enactment which would otherwise govern the transfer of those proceedings, or any part of them.

(8) For the purposes of subsections (3), (4) and (5) there are three levels of court, that is to say the High Court, any county court and any magistrates' court.

(9) The Lord Chancellor may by order make provision for the principal registry of the Family Division of the High Court to be treated as if it were a county court for specified purposes of this Act, or of any provision made under this Act.

(10) Any order under subsection (9) may make such provision as the Lord Chancellor thinks expedient for the purpose of applying (with or without modifications) provisions which apply in relation to the procedure in county courts to the principal registry when it acts as if it were a county court.

(11) In this section "specified" means specified by an order under this section.

(12) Any power of the Lord Chancellor to make an order under this section shall be exercisable by statutory instrument and any statutory instrument containing such an order shall be subject to annulment in pursuance of a resolution of either House of Parliament.

Magistrates' courts.

1980 c. 43.

23.—(1) Proceedings under this Act shall be treated as family proceedings in relation to magistrates' courts.

(2) Subsection (1) is subject to the provisions of section 65(1) and (2) of the Magistrates' Courts Act 1980 (proceedings which may be treated as not being family proceedings), as amended by this Act.

(3) A magistrates' court shall not be competent to entertain any application, or make any order, involving any disputed question as to a party's entitlement to occupy any property by virtue of a beneficial

Subsections (9) and (10)

4.   These subsections provide that an order may be made, as the Lord Chancellor thinks expedient, for the principal registry of the Family Division of the High Court to be treated as if it were a county court.

Subsection (12)

5.   This provides that the orders made under this clause shall be subject to a negative resolution by either House of Parliament.

Clause 23

1.   This clause deals with the powers of the magistrates' courts under this Bill.

Subsections (1) and (2)

2.   These subsections provide that proceedings under this Bill are to be treated as family proceedings in relation to magistrate's courts, except as otherwise provided in subsection (2).

Subsection (3)

2.   This subsection provides that magistrates' courts will not have power to determine property disputes.   It implements the recommendation in paragraph 5.4 of the report.

estate or interest or by virtue of any enactment giving him or her the right to remain in occupation, unless it is unnecessary to determine the question in order to deal with the application or make the order.

(4) A magistrates' court may decline jurisdiction in any proceedings under this Act if it considers that the case can more conveniently be dealt with by another court.

1980 c. 43.

(5) The powers of a magistrates' court under section 63(2) of the Magistrates' Courts Act 1980 to suspend or rescind orders shall not apply in relation to any order made under this Act.

Rules of court.

24.—(1) An authority having power to make rules of court may make such provision for giving effect to—

(a) this Act,

(b) the provisions of any statutory instrument made under this Act, or

(c) any amendment made by this Act in any other enactment,

as appears to that authority to be necessary or expedient.

(2) The rules may, in particular, make provision—

(a) with respect to the procedure to be followed in any proceedings under this Act (including the manner in which any application is to be made or other proceedings commenced);

(b) with respect to the documents and information to be furnished, and notices to be given, in connection with any such proceedings;

(c) with respect to the service of—

(i) notice of any such proceedings, or

(ii) further notices or documents in connection with such proceedings,

including service outside the United Kingdom;

(d) with respect to the period of notice of proceedings under this Act to be given to any party, including the period of notice in cases where any party is outside the United Kingdom;

(e) enabling the court, in such circumstances as may be prescribed, to proceed on any application under this Act even though the respondent has not been given notice of the proceedings;

(f) for the exercise by magistrates' courts, in such circumstances as may be prescribed, of such powers as may be prescribed (even though a party to the proceedings in question is outside England and Wales);

(g) authorising a single justice to discharge the functions of a magistrates' court with respect to such proceedings under this Act as may be prescribed;

(h) authorising a magistrates' court to order any of the parties to such proceedings under this Act as may be prescribed, in such circumstances as may be prescribed, to pay the whole or part of the costs of all or any of the other parties;

Subsection (4)

3.   This subsection provides for the magistrates to be able to decline jurisdiction in any proceedings under this Bill.

Clause 24

1.   This clause gives an enabling power to the relevant rule-making authority to make rules in respect of the procedural requirements of a number of provisions in this Bill.

(j) applying with or without modifications enactments governing the procedure to be followed in any court to proceedings under this Act, or excluding the application of such enactments to such proceedings.

(3) In subsection (2)—

"notice of proceedings" means a summons or such other notice of proceedings as may be required, and "given", in relation to a summons, means served, and

"prescribed" means prescribed by the rules.

(4) This section is not be taken as in any way limiting any other power of the authority in question to make rules of court.

(5) When making any rules under this section an authority shall be subject to the same requirements as to consultation (if any) as apply when the authority makes rules under its general rule-making power.

Appeals.

25.—(1) An appeal shall lie to the High Court against—

(a) the making by a magistrates' court of any order under this Act, or

(b) any refusal by a magistrates' court to make such an order,

but no appeal shall lie against any exercise by a magistrates' court of the power conferred by section 23(4).

(2) On an appeal under this section, the High Court may make such orders as may be necessary to give effect to its determination of the appeal.

(3) Where an order is made under subsection (2) the High Court may also make such incidental or consequential orders as appear to it to be just.

(4) Any order of the High Court made on an appeal under this section (other than one directing that an application be re-heard by a magistrates' court) shall, for the purposes—

(a) of the enforcement of the order, and

(b) of any power to vary, revive or discharge orders,

be treated as if it were an order of the magistrates' court from which the appeal was brought and not an order of the High Court.

(5) The Lord Chancellor may by order made by statutory instrument make provision as to the circumstances in which appeals may be made against decisions taken by courts on questions arising in connection with the transfer, or proposed transfer, of proceedings by virtue of any order under section 22(5).

(6) Except to the extent provided for in any order made under subsection (5), no appeal may be made against any decision of a kind mentioned in that subsection.

(7) A statutory instrument containing an order under subsection (5) shall be subject to annulment in pursuance of a resolution of either House of Parliament.

EXPLANATORY NOTES

Clause 25

1.   This clause deals with the jurisdiction of courts to hear appeals.

General

Meaning of "family proceedings".

26.—(1) In this Act "family proceedings" means any proceedings—

(a) under the inherent jurisdiction of the High Court in relation to children; and

(b) under the enactments mentioned in subsection (2).

(2) Those enactments are—

1973 c. 18   (a) the Matrimonial Causes Act 1973;

1976 c. 36.   (b) the Adoption Act 1976;

1978 c. 22.   (c) the Domestic Proceedings and Magistrates' Courts Act 1978;

1984 c. 42.   (d) Part III of the Matrimonial and Family Proceedings Act 1984;

1989 c. 41.   (e) Parts I, II and IV of the Children Act 1989;

1990 c. 37.   (f) section 30 of the Human Fertilisation and Embryology Act 1990;

(g) this Act.

Interpretation.

27.—(1) In this Act, unless a contrary intention appears—

"associated", in relation to a person, shall be construed in accordance with section 2,

"child" means a person under the age of eighteen years,

"cohabitant" and "former cohabitant" shall be construed in accordance with section 1,

"the court" shall be construed in accordance with section 22,

"dwelling-house" includes any building or part of a building which is occupied as a dwelling, and any yard, garden, garage or outhouse belonging to the dwelling-house and occupied with it,

"family proceedings" has the meaning given by section 26,

"harm"—

(a) in relation to a child, has the same meaning as in section 31 of the Children Act 1989, and

(b) in relation to any other person, means ill-treatment or the impairment of physical or mental health,

"matrimonial home rights" has the meaning given by section 4,

1925 c. 20.   "mortgage", "mortgagor" and "mortgagee" have the same meaning as in the Law of Property Act 1925,

"mortgage payments" includes any payments which, under the terms of the mortgage, the mortgagor is required to make to any person,

"non-molestation order" has the meaning given by section 13(1),

"occupation order" has the meaning given by section 11,

"parental responsibility" has the same meaning as in the Children Act 1989,

"relative", in relation to a person, means—

(a) the father, mother, stepfather, stepmother, son, daughter, stepson, stepdaughter, grandmother, grandfather, grandson or granddaughter of that person or of that person's spouse or former spouse, or

EXPLANATORY NOTES

Clause 26

1.   This clause defines "family proceedings" for the purposes of this Bill.   The definition is the same as that used in section 8(4) of the Children Act 1989.

Clause 27

Subsection (1)

1.   This is the interpretation clause and, inter alia, provides a definition of "relative" for the purposes of clause 2(d) and "harm" for the purposes of clauses 7, 9 and 10 above. This is discussed in paragraph 4.34 of the report.

Subsection (2)

2.   This subsection makes it clear that the Bill will apply to a husband and wife who entered into marriage under a law which permits polygamy.

(b) the brother, sister, uncle, aunt, niece or nephew (whether of the full blood or of the half blood or by affinity) of that person or of that person's spouse or former spouse,

and includes, in relation to a person who is living or has lived with another person as husband and wife, any person who would fall within paragraph (a) or (b) if the parties were married to each other, and

"relevant child", in relation to any proceedings under this Act, has the meaning given by section 3.

(2) It is hereby declared that this Act applies as between a husband and a wife notwithstanding that the marriage in question was entered into under a law which permits polygamy (whether or not either party to the marriage in question has for the time being any spouse additional to the other party).

Consequential amendments and repeals.

28.—(1) The enactments specified in Schedule 5 shall have effect subject to the amendments specified in that Schedule.

(2) The transitional provisions and savings in Schedule 6 shall have effect.

(2) The enactments specified in Schedule 7 are hereby repealed to the extent specified in the third column of that Schedule.

Short title, commencement and extent.

29.—(1) This Act may be cited as the Family Homes and Domestic Violence Act 1992.

(2) This Act shall come into force on such day as the Lord Chancellor may by order appoint.

(3) This Act extends to England and Wales only.

EXPLANATORY NOTES

Clause 28

1.   This clause deals with consequential amendments, transitional provisions and repeals. It gives effect to Schedules 5, 6 and 7 of the Bill which deal with these matters.

Clause 29

1.   This clause deals with the commencement, short title and extent of this Bill.

SCHEDULES

Section 6.

SCHEDULE 1

PROVISIONS SUPPLEMENTARY TO SECTIONS 4 AND 5

Interpretation

1. In this Schedule—

1985 c. 61.

(a) any reference to a solicitor includes a reference to a licensed conveyancer as defined in section 11(2) of the Administration of Justice Act 1985 or a recognised body as defined in section 39(1) of that Act, and

(b) any reference to a person's solicitor includes a reference to a licensed conveyancer or recognised body acting for that person.

Restriction on registration where spouse entitled to more than one charge

2. Where one spouse is entitled by virtue of section 5 to a registrable charge in respect of each of two or more dwelling-houses, only one of the charges to which that spouse is so entitled shall be

1972 c. 61.

registered under section 2 of the Land Charges Act 1972 or section 5(6) of this Act at any one time, and if any of those charges is registered under either of those provisions the Chief Land Registrar, on being satisfied that any other of them is so registered, shall cancel the registration of the charge first registered.

Contract for sale of house affected by registered charge to include term requiring cancellation of registration before completion.

3.—(1) Where one spouse is entitled by virtue of section 5 to a charge on an estate in a dwelling-house and the charge is registered under section 2 of the Land Charges Act 1972 or section 5(6) of this Act, it shall be a term of any contract for the sale of that estate whereby the vendor agrees to give vacant possession of the dwelling-house on completion of the contract that the vendor will before such completion procure the cancellation of the registration of the charge at his own expense.

(2) Sub-paragraph (1) shall not apply to any such contract made by a vendor who is entitled to sell the estate in the dwelling-house freed from any such charge.

(3) If, on the completion of such a contract as is referred to in sub-paragraph (1), there is delivered to the purchaser or his solicitor an application by the spouse entitled to the charge for the cancellation of the registration of that charge, the term of the contract for which sub-paragraph (1) provides shall be deemed to have been performed.

(4) This paragraph applies only if and so far as a contrary intention is not expressed in the contract.

EXPLANATORY NOTES

THE SCHEDULES

Schedule 1

1.   This Schedule reproduces, with consequential amendments, sections 3,4,5 and 6 of the Matrimonial Homes Act 1983. These sections dealt with conveyancing aspects of a spouse's rights of occupation in the matrimonial home. The other sections of the 1983 Act are reproduced or replaced in the substantive part of this Bill. The Schedule uses the term "matrimonial home rights" in place of "rights of occupation" which was used in the 1983 Act.

2.   Paragraph 1 provides for the interpretation of various expressions used in this Schedule.

3.   Paragraph 2 reproduces section 3 of the 1983 Act. It provides that where a spouse is entitled to a registrable charge in respect of each of two or more dwelling-houses, only one of those charges may be registered. If more than one charge is registered the Chief Registrar must cancel the registration of the charge first registered.

4.   Paragraph 3 reproduces section 4 of the 1983 Act, without substantive change. It protects the purchaser of a dwelling-house in respect of which the vendor's spouse is entitled to matrimonial home rights by making it an implied term of the contract that the vendor will procure cancellation of any registered charge in any case where vacant possession is to be given on completion.

(5) This paragraph shall apply to a contract for exchange as it applies to a contract for sale.

(6) This paragraph shall, with the necessary modifications, apply to a contract for the grant of a lease or underlease of a dwelling-house as it applies to a contract for the sale of an estate in a dwelling-house.

Cancellation of registration after termination of marriage, etc.

1972 c. 61.

4.—(1) Where a spouse's rights of occupation are a charge on an estate in the dwelling-house and the charge is registered under section 2 of the Land Charges Act 1972 or section 5(6) of this Act, the Chief Land Registrar shall, subject to sub-paragraph (2), cancel the registration of the charge if he is satisfied—

(a) by the production of a certificate or other sufficient evidence, that either spouse is dead, or

(b) by the production of an official copy of a decree of a court, that the marriage in question has been terminated otherwise than by death, or

(c) by the production of an order of the court, that the spouse's matrimonial home rights constituting the charge have been terminated by the order.

(2) Where—

(a) the marriage in question has been terminated by the death of the spouse entitled to an estate in the dwelling-house or otherwise than by death, and

(b) an order affecting the charge of the spouse not so entitled had been made by virtue of section 7(4),

then if, after the making of the order, registration of the charge was renewed or the charge registered in pursuance of sub-paragraph (3), the Chief Land Registrar shall not cancel the registration of the charge in accordance with sub-paragraph (1) unless he is also satisfied that the order has ceased to have effect.

(3) Where such an order has been made, then, for the purposes of sub-paragraph (2), the spouse entitled to the charge affected by the order may—

(a) if before the date of the order the charge was registered under section 2 of the Land Charges Act 1972 or section 5(6) of this Act, renew the registration of the charge, and

(b) if before the said date the charge was not so registered, register the charge under section 2 of the Land Charges Act 1972 or section 5(6) of this Act.

(4) Renewal of the registration of a charge in pursuance of sub-paragraph (3) shall be effected in such manner as may be prescribed, and an application for such renewal or for registration of a charge in pursuance of that sub-paragraph shall contain such particulars of any order affecting the charge made by virtue of section 7(4) as may be prescribed.

(5) The renewal in pursuance of sub-paragraph (3) of the registration of a charge shall not affect the priority of the charge.

5.   Paragraph 4 reproduces section 5 of the 1983 Act without substantive change.   It provides for the cancellation of registered charges after the termination of the marriage and for the renewal of registration in cases where an order has been made under clause 7(4) above extending matrimonial home rights beyond the end of the marriage.

(6) In this paragraph "prescribed" means prescribed by rules made under section 16 of the Land Charges Act 1972 or section 144 of the Land Registration Act 1925, as the circumstances of the case require.

Release of matrimonial home rights

5.—(1) A spouse entitled to matrimonial home rights may by a release in writing release those rights or release them as respects part only of the dwelling-house affected by them.

(2) Where a contract is made for the sale of an estate or interest in a dwelling-house, or for the grant of a lease or underlease of a dwelling-house, being (in either case) a dwelling-house affected by a charge registered under section 2 of the Land Charges Act 1972 or section 5(6) of this Act, then, without prejudice to sub-paragraph (1), the matrimonial homes rights constituting the charge shall be deemed to have been released on the happening of whichever of the following events first occurs—

(a) the delivery to the purchaser or lessee, as the case may be, or his solicitor on completion of the contract of an application by the spouse entitled to the charge for the cancellation of the registration of the charge, or

(b) the lodging of such an application at Her Majesty's Land Registry.

Postponement of priority of charge

6. A spouse entitled by virtue of section 5 to a charge on an estate or interest may agree in writing that any other charge on, or interest in, that estate or interest shall rank in priority to the charge to which that spouse is so entitled.

SCHEDULE 2

POWERS OF HIGH COURT AND COUNTY COURT TO REMAND

Interpretation

1. In this Schedule "the court" means the High Court or a county court and includes—

(a) in relation to the High Court, a judge of that court, and

(b) in relation to a county court, a judge or district judge of that court.

Remand in custody or on bail

2.—(1) Where a court has power to remand a person under section 15, the court may—

(a) remand him in custody, that is to say, commit him to custody to be brought before the court at the end of the period of remand or at such earlier time as the court may require, or

(b) remand him on bail—

(i) by taking from him a recognizance (with or without sureties) conditioned as provided in sub-paragraph (3), or

EXPLANATORY NOTES

6.   Paragraphs 5 and 6 are derived from section 6 of the 1983 Act. These paragraphs enable a spouse to postpone his registered charge to that of another person or to release it altogether.

Schedule 2

1.   This Schedule establishes a scheme for the remand of persons arrested pursuant to a power of arrest or warrant granted by the High Court and county courts. It is based on the existing scheme in the magistrates' courts established by sections 128 and 129 of the Magistrates' Courts Act 1980.

2.   Paragraphs 2, 3 and 4 provide that the court may remand the person arrested either in custody or on bail by taking a recognizance and imposes certain time limits.

(ii) by fixing the amount of the recognizances with a view to their being taken subsequently in accordance with paragraph 4 and in the meantime committing the person to custody in accordance with paragraph (a).

(2) Where a person is brought before the court after remand, the court may further remand him.

(3) Where a person is remanded on bail under sub-paragraph (1), the court may direct that his recognizance be conditioned for his appearance—

(a) before that court at the end of the period of remand, or

(b) at every time and place to which during the course of the proceedings the hearing may from time to time be adjourned.

(4) Where a recognizance is conditioned for a person's appearance in accordance with sub-paragraph (1)(b), the fixing of any time for him next to appear shall be deemed to be a remand; but nothing in this sub-paragraph or sub-paragraph (3) shall deprive the court of power at any subsequent hearing to remand him afresh.

(5) Subject to paragraph 3, the court shall not remand a person under this paragraph for a period exceeding 8 clear days, except that—

(a) if the court remands him on bail, it may remand him for a longer period if he and the other party consent, and

(b) if the court adjourns a case under section 16(1), the court may remand him for the period of the adjournment.

(6) Where the court has power under this paragraph to remand a person in custody it may, if the remand is for a period not exceeding 3 clear days, commit him to the custody of a constable.

Further remand

3.—(1) If the court is satisfied that any person who has been remanded under paragraph 2 is unable by reason of illness or accident to appear or be brought before the court at the expiration of the period for which he was remanded, the court may, in his absence, remand him for a further time; and paragraph 2(5) shall not apply.

(2) Notwithstanding anything in paragraph 2(1), the power of the court under sub-paragraph (1) to remand a person on bail for a further time may be exercised by enlarging his recognizance and those of any sureties for him to a later time.

(3) Where a person remanded on bail under paragraph 2 is bound to appear before the court at any time and the court has no power to remand him under sub-paragraph (1), the court may in his absence enlarge his recognizance and those of any sureties for him to a later time; and the enlargement of his recognizance shall be deemed to be a further remand.

Postponement of taking of recognizance

4. Where under paragraph 2(1)(b)(ii) the court fixes the amount in which the principal and his sureties, if any, are to be bound, the recognizance may thereafter be taken by such person as may be prescribed by rules of court, and the same consequences shall follow as if it had been entered into before the court.

Section 18.

SCHEDULE 3

AMENDMENTS OF CHILDREN ACT 1989

1989 c. 41.

1. After section 38 of the Children Act 1989 there is inserted—

"Power to include exclusion requirement in interim care order.

38A.—(1) Where—

    (a) on being satisfied that there are reasonable grounds for believing that the circumstances with respect to a child are as mentioned in section 31(2)(a) and (b)(i), the court makes an interim care order with respect to a child, and

    (b) the conditions mentioned in subsection (2) are satisfied,

the court may include an exclusion requirement in the interim care order.

(2) The conditions are—

    (a) that there is reasonable cause to believe that, if a person ("the relevant person") is excluded from a dwelling-house in which the child lives, the child will cease to suffer, or cease to be likely to suffer, significant harm, and

    (b) that another person living in the dwelling-house (whether a parent of the child or some other person)—

        (i) is able and willing to give to the child the care which it would be reasonable to expect a parent to give him, and

        (ii) consents to the order being made.

(3) For the purposes of this section an exclusion requirement is any one or more of the following—

    (a) a provision requiring the relevant person to leave a dwelling-house in which he is living with the child,

    (b) a provision prohibiting the relevant person from entering a dwelling-house in which the child lives, and

    (b) a provision excluding the relevant person from a defined area in which a dwelling-house in which the child lives is situated.

EXPLANATORY NOTES

Schedule 3

1.   This Schedule makes amendments to the Children Act 1989.   These are intended to enable the court to make an ouster order for the protection of children which will permit the removal of a suspected abuser from the home instead of having to remove the child under an emergency protection or interim care order. This implements the recommendation in paragraph 6.17 of the report.

2.   Paragraph 1 inserts a new section 38A into the Children Act 1989. This implements the recommendation in paragraph 6.17 of the report in relation to interim care orders.

Subsections 38A(1) (2) and (3)
These provide that if the criteria for making an interim care order under the 1989 Act are satisfied and there is reasonable cause to believe that the likelihood of harm to the child will not arise if the suspected person is excluded from a particular dwelling-house, then an order may be made ousting or prohibiting the suspected person from that dwelling-house or from its vicinity.   There must also be another person in the household who is willing and able to provide reasonable care for the child and consents to the order being made.   This implements the recommendation in paragraph 6.18 of the report.

SCH. 3

(4) The court may provide that the exclusion requirement is to have effect for a shorter period than the other provisions of the interim care order.

(5) Where the court makes an interim care order containing an exclusion requirement, the court may attach a power of arrest to the exclusion requirement.

(6) Where a power of arrest is attached to an exclusion requirement of an interim care order by virtue of subsection (5), a constable may arrest without warrant any person whom he has reasonable cause to believe to be in breach of the requirement.

(7) Sections 15(5) and 16 of, and Schedule 2 to, the Family Homes and Domestic Violence Act 1992 shall have effect in relation to a person arrested under subsection (6) of this section as they have effect in relation to a person arrested under section 15(4) of that Act.

(8) If, while an interim care order containing an exclusion requirement is in force, the local authority remove the child from the dwelling-house from which the relevant person is excluded, the order shall cease to have effect in so far as it imposes the exclusion requirement."

1989 c. 41.

2. In section 39 of the Children Act 1989 (discharge and variation etc. of care orders and supervision orders) after subsection (3) there is inserted—

"(3A) On the application of an person who is not entitled to apply for the order to be discharged, but who is a person to whom an exclusion requirement contained in the order applies, an interim care order may be varied or discharged by the court in so far as it imposes the exclusion requirement."

3. After section 44 of the Children Act 1989 there is inserted—

"Power to include exclusion requirement in emergency protection order.

44A.—(1) Where—

(a) on being satisfied as mentioned in section 44(1)(a), (b) or (c), the court makes an emergency protection order with respect to a child, and

(b) the conditions mentioned in subsection (2) are satisfied,

the court may include an exclusion requirement in the emergency protection order.

(2) The conditions are—

(a) that there is reasonable cause to believe that, if a person ("the relevant person") is excluded from a dwelling-house in which the child lives, then—

(i) in the case of an order made on the ground mentioned in section 44(1)(a), the child will not be likely to suffer significant

Subsection 38A(4)

This subsection enables the court to specify a shorter duration period for the ouster order than for the interim care order. It implements the recommendation in paragraph 6.21 of the report.

Subsections 38A(5), (6) and (7)

These subsections give the court power to attach a power of arrest to an ouster order and apply the relevant provisions of this Bill to such a power. This implements the recommendation in paragraph 6.22 of the report.

Subsection 38A(8)

This subsection provides that the ouster order will lapse automatically if the local authority removes the child from the dwelling-house concerned. This implements the recommendation in paragraph 6.19 of the report.

3.   Paragraph 2 inserts a new subsection (3A) in section 39 of the 1989 Act. This ensures that the parties would have the same right to challenge the ouster order as they have to challenge the interim care order to which it is supplementary.

4.   Paragraph 3 inserts a new section 44A into the 1989 Act. This implements the recommendation made in paragraph 6.17 of the report in relation to emergency protection orders.

Subsections 44A(1), (2) and (3)

These provide that if the criteria for making an emergency protection order under the 1989 Act are satisfied and there is reasonable cause to believe that the likelihood of harm to the child will not arise, or that the investigating authorities' access to the child's home will no longer be frustrated, if the suspected person is excluded from the dwelling-house, then an order may be made ousting or prohibiting the suspected person from that dwelling-house or from its vicinity. There must also be another person in the household who is willing and able to provide reasonable care for the child and consents to the order being made.

harm, even though the child is not removed as mentioned in section 44(1)(a)(i) or does not remain as mentioned in section 44(1)(a)(ii), or

(ii) in the case of an order made on the ground mentioned in paragraph (b) or (c) of section 44(1), the enquiries referred to in that paragraph will cease to be frustrated, and

(b) that another person living in the dwelling-house (whether a parent of the child or some other person)—

(i) is able and willing to give to the child the care which it would be reasonable to expect a parent to give him, and

(ii) consents to the order being made.

(3) For the purposes of this section an exclusion requirement is any one or more of the following—

(a) a provision requiring the relevant person to leave a dwelling-house in which he is living with the child

(b) a provision prohibiting the relevant person from entering a dwelling-house in which the child lives, and

(b) a provision excluding the relevant person from a defined area in which a dwelling-house in which the child lives is situated.

(4) Subsections (4) to (7) of section 38A shall have effect in relation to an emergency protection order as they have effect in relation to an interim care order.

(5) If, while an emergency protection order containing an exclusion requirement is in force, the applicant exercises the power given by section 44(4)(b)(i), the order shall cease to have effect in so far as it imposes the exclusion requirement."

4. In section 45 of the Children Act 1989 (duration of emergency protection orders and other supplemental provisions) after subsection (8) there is inserted—

"(8A) On the application of a person who is not entitled to apply for the order to be discharged, but who is a person to whom an exclusion requirement contained in the order applies, an emergency protection order may be varied or discharged by the court in so far as it imposes the exclusion requirement."

Subsection 44A(4)

This subsection applies the provisions relating to duration and powers of arrest to ouster orders made supplementary to emergency protection orders as they apply to those made supplementary to interim care orders. It implements the recommendations made in paragraphs 6.21 and 6.22 of the report.

Subsection 44A(5)

This subsection provides that the ouster order will lapse automatically if the child is removed from the dwelling-house concerned under the emergency protection order. It implements the recommendation made in paragraph 6.19 of the report.

5.   Paragraph 4 inserts a new subsection (8A) in section 45 of the 1989 Act. This ensures that the parties have the same right to challenge the ouster order as they have to challenge the emergency protection order to which it is supplementary.

Section 19.

SCHEDULE 4

TRANSFER OF CERTAIN TENANCIES ON DIVORCE ETC. OR ON SEPARATION OF COHABITANTS

PART I

GENERAL

Interpretation

1. In this Schedule—

"cohabitant", except in paragraph 3, includes where the context requires former cohabitant,

"the court" does not include a magistrates' court,

"landlord" includes any person from time to time deriving title under the original landlord and also includes, in relation to any dwelling-house, any person other than the tenant who is, or but for Part VII of the Rent Act 1977 or Part II of the Rent (Agriculture) Act 1976 would be, entitled to possession of the dwelling-house,

"a relevant tenancy" means—

(a) a protected tenancy or statutory tenancy within the meaning of the Rent Act 1977,

(b) a statutory tenancy within the meaning of the Rent (Agriculture) Act 1976,

(c) a secure tenancy within the meaning of section 79 of the Housing Act 1985, or

(d) an assured tenancy or assured agricultural occupancy within the meaning of Part I of the Housing Act 1988,

"spouse", except in paragraph 2, includes where the context requires former spouse, and

"tenancy" includes sub-tenancy.

1977 c. 42.
1976 c. 80.

1985 c. 68.

1988 c. 50

Cases in which court may make order

2. Where one spouse is entitled, either in his own right or jointly with the other spouse, to occupy a dwelling-house by virtue of a relevant tenancy, then, on granting a decree of divorce, a decree of nullity of marriage or a decree of judicial separation or at any time thereafter (whether, in the case of a decree of divorce or nullity of marriage, before or after the decree is made absolute), the court by which the decree is granted may make an order under Part II of this Schedule.

3. Where one cohabitant is entitled, either in his own right or jointly with the other cohabitant, to occupy a dwelling-house by virtue of a relevant tenancy and the cohabitants cease to live together as husband and wife, then, at any time after they cease so to live together, the court may make an order under Part II of this Schedule.

4. The court shall not make an order under Part II of this Schedule unless the dwelling-house is or was—

(a) in the case of spouses, a matrimonial home, or

EXPLANATORY NOTES

Schedule 4

1.   This Schedule deals with the transfer of certain tenancies following divorce or on the separation of cohabitants. The Schedule is derived from Schedule 1 of the Matrimonial Homes Act 1983, but has been extended to enable orders to be made between cohabitants as well as spouses. It implements the recommendation in paragraph 6.6 of the report.

2.   Paragraph 1 provides for the interpretation of various expressions used in the Schedule.

3.   Paragraph 2 reproduces Schedule 1 paragraph 1(1) of the 1983 Act.

4.   Paragraph 3 empowers the court to make a transfer of a relevant tenancy between cohabitants who have ceased to live together as husband and wife.

5.   Paragraph 4 makes it clear that a transfer can only be made in respect of a matrimonial home or, in the case of cohabitants, a house in which they have lived together as husband and wife.

SCH. 4

(b) in the case of cohabitants, a home in which they lived together as husband and wife.

Matters to which court must have regard

5. In determining whether to exercise its powers under Part II of this Schedule and, if so, in what manner, the court shall have regard to all the circumstances of the case including—

(a) the circumstances in which the tenancy was granted to either or both of the spouses or cohabitants or, as the case requires, the circumstances in which either or both of them became tenant under the tenancy,

(b) the matters mentioned in section 7(5)(a), (b) and (c) and, where the parties are cohabitants and only one of them is entitled to occupy the dwelling-house by virtue of the relevant tenancy, the further matters mentioned in section 9(4)(a) and (b), and

(c) the respective suitability of the parties as tenants.

PART II

ORDERS THAT MAY BE MADE

References to entitlement to occupy

6. References in this Part of this Schedule to a spouse or a cohabitant being entitled to occupy a dwelling-house by virtue of a relevant tenancy apply whether that entitlement is in his own right or jointly with the other spouse or cohabitant.

Protected, secure or assured tenancy or assured agricultural occupancy

1977 c. 42.
1985 c. 68.
1988 c. 50

7.—(1) Where a spouse or cohabitant is entitled to occupy the dwelling-house by virtue of a protected tenancy within the meaning of the Rent Act 1977, a secure tenancy within the meaning of the Housing Act 1985 or an assured tenancy or assured agricultural occupancy within the meaning of Part I of the Housing Act 1988, the court may by order direct that, as from such date as may be specified in the order, there shall, by virtue of the order and without further assurance, be transferred to, and vested in, the other spouse or cohabitant—

(a) the estate or interest which the spouse or cohabitant so entitled had in the dwelling-house immediately before that date by virtue of the lease or agreement creating the tenancy and any assignment of that lease of agreement, with all rights, privileges and appurtenances attaching to that estate or interest but subject to all covenants, obligations, liabilities and incumbrances to which it is subject, and

(b) where the spouse or cohabitant so entitled is an assignee of such lease or agreement, the liability of that spouse or cohabitant under any covenant of indemnity by the assignee express or implied in the assignment of the lease or agreement to that spouse or cohabitant.

6.   Paragraph 5 sets out the criteria which the court must apply when deciding whether to make an order. This implements the recommendation in paragraph 6.9 of the report.

7.   Part II of this Schedule describes the orders which can be made by a court under this Schedule.

8.   Paragraph 6 makes it clear that any references to a spouse or a cohabitant being entitled to occupy apply whether the entitlement is in his own right or jointly with the other spouse or cohabitant.

9.   Paragraph 7 is derived from Schedule 1 paragraph 2 of the 1983 Act. Its provisions have been extended to cover cohabitants as well as spouses.

SCH. 4

(2) Where an order is made under this paragraph, any liability or obligation to which the spouse or cohabitant so entitled is subject under any covenant having reference to the dwelling-house in the lease or agreement, being a liability or obligation falling due to be discharged or performed on or after the date so specified, shall not be enforceable against that spouse or cohabitant.

1985 c. 68.

(3) Where the spouse so entitled is a successor within the meaning of Part IV of the Housing Act 1985, his former spouse or former cohabitant (or, in the case of judicial separation, his spouse) shall be deemed also to be a successor within the meaning of that Chapter.

1988 c. 50.

(4) Where the spouse or cohabitant so entitled is for the purpose of section 17 of the Housing Act 1988 a successor in relation to the tenancy or occupancy, his former spouse or former cohabitant (or, in the case of judicial separation, his spouse) shall be deemed to be a successor in relation to the tenancy or occupation for the purposes of that section.

(5) If the transfer under sub-paragraph (1) is of an assured agricultural occupancy, then, for the purposes of Chapter III of Part I of the Housing Act 1988—

(a) the agricultural worker condition shall be fulfilled with respect to the dwelling-house while the spouse or cohabitant to whom the assured agricultural occupancy is transferred continues to be the occupier under that occupancy, and

(b) that condition shall be treated as so fulfilled by virtue of the same paragraph of Schedule 3 to the Housing Act 1988 as was applicable before the transfer.

Statutory tenancy within the meaning of the Rent Act 1977

1977 c. 42.

8.—(1) Where the spouse or cohabitant is entitled to occupy the dwelling-house by virtue of a statutory tenancy within the meaning of the Rent Act 1977, the court may by order direct that, as from the date specified in the order, that spouse or cohabitant shall cease to be entitled to occupy the dwelling-house and that the other spouse or cohabitant shall be deemed to be the tenant or, as the case may be, the sole tenant under that statutory tenancy.

(2) The question whether the provisions of paragraphs 1 to 3 or, as the case may be, paragraphs 5 to 7 of Schedule 1 to the Rent Act 1977 as to the succession by the surviving spouse of a deceased tenant, or by a member of the deceased tenant's family, to the right to retain possession are capable of having effect in the event of the death of the person deemed by an order under this paragraph to be the tenant or sole tenant under the statutory tenancy shall be determined according as those provisions have or have not already had effect in relation to the statutory tenancy.

10.   Paragraph 8 extends the present provisions of paragraph 3 of Schedule 1 of the 1983 Act by providing for transfers between cohabitants in addition to spouses.

Statutory tenancy within the meaning of the Rent (Agriculture) Act 1976

9. Where the spouse or cohabitant is entitled to occupy the dwelling-house by virtue of a statutory tenancy within the meaning of the Rent (Agriculture) Act 1976, the court may by order direct that, as from such date as may be specified in the order, that spouse or cohabitant shall cease to be entitled to occupy the dwelling-house and that the other spouse or cohabitant shall be deemed to be the tenant or, as the case may be, the sole tenant under that statutory tenancy; and a spouse who is deemed under this paragraph to be the tenant under a statutory tenancy shall be (within the meaning of that Act) a statutory tenant in his own right, or a statutory tenant by succession, according as the other spouse was a statutory tenant in his own right or a statutory tenant by succession.

PART III

SUPPLEMENTARY PROVISIONS

Compensation

10.—(1) Where the court makes an order under Part II of this Schedule, it may by the order direct the making of a payment by the spouse or cohabitant to whom the tenancy is transferred ("the transferee") to the other spouse or cohabitant ("the transferor").

(2) In deciding whether to exercise its powers under this paragraph and, if so, in what manner, the court shall have regard to all the circumstances including—

(a) the financial loss that would otherwise be suffered by the transferor as a result of the order,

(b) the financial resources of the parties, and

(c) the financial obligations which the parties have, or are likely to have in the foreseeable future, including financial obligations to each other or to any relevant child.

Liabilities and obligations in respect of the dwelling-house

11. Where the court makes an order under Part II of this Schedule, it may by the order direct that both spouses or cohabitants shall be jointly and severally liable to discharge or perform any or all of the liabilities and obligations in respect of the dwelling-house (whether arising under the tenancy or otherwise) which have at the date of the order fallen due to be discharged or performed by one only of them or which, but for the direction, would before the date specified as the date on which the order is to take effect fall due to be discharged or performed by one only of them; and where the court gives such a direction it may further direct that either spouse or cohabitant shall be liable to indemnify the other in whole or in part against any payment made or expenses incurred by the other in discharging or performing any such liability or obligation.

11.   Paragraph 9 is derived from Schedule 1 paragraph 4 of the 1983 Act which is extended to cover transfers between cohabitants.

12.   Part III of this Schedule deals with provisions supplementary to an order for a transfer of a tenancy.

13.   Paragraph 10 gives the court power to order one party to compensate the other for any financial loss suffered as a consequence of the tenancy being transferred to the other spouse or cohabitant. This implements the recommendation in paragraph 6.12 of the report. Paragraph 10(2) directs the court, when considering compensation, to have particular regard to the financial loss to the transferor if no compensation is awarded, the parties' financial needs and resources and any financial obligations which the parties have or are likely to have in the foreseeable future.

14.   Paragraph 11 reproduces the provisions of paragraph 5 of Schedule 1 of the 1983 Act, and extends them to cohabitants.

Date when order made between spouses is to take effect

12. In the case of a decree of divorce or nullity of marriage, the date specified in an order under Part II of this Schedule as the date on which the order is to take effect shall not be earlier than the date on which the decree is made absolute.

Remarriage of either spouse

13.—(1) If after the grant of a decree dissolving or annulling a marriage either spouse remarries, that spouse shall not be entitled to apply, by reference to the grant of that decree, for an order under Part II of this Schedule.

(2) For the avoidance of doubt it is hereby declared that the reference in sub-paragraph (1) to remarriage includes a reference to a marriage which is by law void or voidable.

Rules of court

14.—(1) Rules of court shall be made requiring the court before it makes an order under this Schedule to give the landlord of the dwelling-house to which the order will relate an opportunity of being heard.

(2) Rules of court may provide that an application for an order under this Schedule by reference to a decree of divorce, nullity of marriage or judicial separation shall not, without the leave of the court by which that decree was granted, be made after the expiration of such period from the grant of the decree as may be prescribed by the rules.

Saving for other provisions of Act

15.—(1) Where a spouse is entitled to occupy a dwelling-house by virtue of a tenancy, this Schedule shall not affect the operation of sections 4 and 5 in relation to the other spouse's matrimonial home rights.

(2) Where a spouse or cohabitant is entitled to occupy a dwelling-house by virtue of a tenancy, the court's powers to make orders under this Schedule shall be in addition to the powers conferred by sections 7 and 9.

Section 28(1).

SCHEDULE 5

CONSEQUENTIAL AMENDMENTS

The Land Registration Act 1925 (c. 21)

1. In section 64 of the Land Registration Act 1925 (certificates to be produced and noted on dealings) in subsection (5) for "section 2(8) of the Matrimonial Homes Act 1983" there is substituted "section 5(6) of the Family Homes and Domestic Violence Act 1992".

15.   Paragraph 12 reproduces paragraph 6 of Schedule 1 of the 1983 Act. It ensures that a transfer order cannot take effect before a decree of divorce or nullity is made absolute.

16.   Paragraph 13(1) reproduces paragraph 7 of Schedule 1 of the 1983 Act. It provides that no spouse can apply for a transfer after remarriage. Paragraph 13(2) derives from paragraph 10(2) of Schedule 1 of the 1983 Act. It makes it clear that a reference to remarriage will include a marriage which is by law void or voidable.

17.   Paragraph 14(1) reproduces paragraph 8(1) of Schedule 1 of the 1983 Act. It provides for rules to be made giving the landlord an opportunity to be heard before a transfer order is made. Paragraph 14(2) reproduces paragraph 8(2) of Schedule 1 of the 1983 Act.

18.   Paragraph 15 makes savings for other provisions of this Bill.

Schedule 5

1.   This Schedule deals with amendments to other enactments consequent upon the provisions of the Bill.

The Matrimonial Causes Act 1973 (c. 18)

2. In section 4(4) of the Matrimonial Causes Act 1973 (cases where court may treat certain periods as periods of desertion) for paragraphs (b) and (c) there is substituted—

"(b) any period during which there is in force an order made by any court under the Family Homes and Domestic Violence Act 1992 (or any of the enactments repealed by that Act) which—

(i) excludes the respondent from a dwelling-house which is, or was at any time, the matrimonial home, or

(ii) prohibits the exercise by the respondent of the right to occupy such a home."

The Magistrates' Courts Act 1980 (c. 43)

3. In section 65(1) of the Magistrates' Courts Act 1980 (meaning of family proceedings) after paragraph (n) there shall be inserted—

"(o) the Family Homes and Domestic Violence Act 1992;".

The Contempt of Court Act 1981 (c. 49)

4. In Schedule 3 to the Contempt of Court Act 1981 (application of Magistrates' Courts Act 1980 to civil contempt proceedings), in paragraph 3 for the words from "'or, having been arrested" onwards there is substituted—

"'or, having been arrested under section 15 of the Family Homes and Domestic Violence Act 1992 in connection with the matter of the complaint, is at large after being remanded under subsection (5)(b) or (8) of that section.'"

The Matrimonial and Family Proceedings Act 1984 (c. 42)

5. For section 22 of the Matrimonial and Family Proceedings Act 1984 there is substituted—

"Powers of court in relation to certain tenancies of dwelling-houses.

22. Where an application is made by a party to a marriage for an order for financial relief then, if one of the parties is entitled, either in his own right or jointly with the other party, to occupy a dwelling-house situated in England or Wales by virtue of a tenancy which is a relevant tenancy within the meaning of Schedule 4 to the Family Homes and Domestic Violence Act 1992 (certain statutory tenancies), the court may make in relation to that dwelling-house any order which it could make under Part II of that Schedule if a decree of divorce, a decree of nullity of marriage or a decree of judicial separation in respect of the marriage had been granted in England and Wales; and the provisions of paragraphs 10, 11 and 14(1) in Part III of that Schedule shall apply in relation to any order made

under this section as they apply to any order made under Part II of that Schedule."

The Housing Act 1985 (c. 68)

6.—(1) Section 85 of the Housing Act 1985 (extended discretion of court in certain proceedings for possession) is amended as follows.

(2) In subsection (5)—

(a) in paragraph (a), for "rights of occupation under the Matrimonial Homes Act 1983" there is substituted "matrimonial home rights under the Family Homes and Domestic Violence Act 1992", and

(b) for "those rights of occupation" there is substituted "those matrimonial home rights".

(3) After subsection (5) there is inserted—

"(5A) Where proceedings are brought for possession of a dwelling-house which is let under a secure tenancy and—

(a) an order is in force under section 9 of the Family Homes and Domestic Violence Act 1992 conferring rights on a cohabitant or former cohabitant (within the meaning of that Act) or former spouse of the tenant,

(b) that cohabitant, former cohabitant or former spouse is then in occupation of the dwelling-house, and

(b) the tenancy is terminated as a result of those proceedings,

the cohabitant, former cohabitant or former spouse shall, so long as he or she remains in occupation, have the same rights in relation to, or in connection with, any adjournment, stay, suspension or postponement in pursuance of this section as he or she would have if the rights conferred by the order referred to in paragraph (a) were not affected by the termination of the tenancy."

7. In section 101 of that Act (rent not to be increased on account of tenant's improvements) in subsection (3) for paragraph (d) there is substituted—

"(d) a spouse, former spouse, cohabitant or former cohabitant of the tenant to whom the tenancy has been transferred by an order made under Schedule 1 to the Matrimonial Homes Act 1983 or Schedule 4 to the Family Homes and Domestic Violence Act 1992."

8. In section 171B of that Act (extent of preserved right to buy: qualifying persons and dwelling-houses) in subsection (4)(b)(ii) after "Schedule 1 to the Matrimonial Homes Act 1983" there is inserted "or Schedule 4 to the Family Homes and Domestic Violence Act 1992".

The Insolvency Act 1986 (c. 45)

9.—(1) Section 336 of the Insolvency Act 1986 (rights of occupation etc. of bankrupt's spouse) is amended as follows.

(2) In subsection (1), for "rights of occupation under the Matrimonial Homes Act 1983" there is substituted "matrimonial home rights under the Family Homes and Domestic Violence Act 1992".

(3) In subsection (2)—

(a) for "rights of occupation under the Act of 1983" there is substituted "matrimonial home rights under the Act of 1992", and

(b) in paragraph (b), for "under section 1 of that Act" there is substituted "under section 7 of that Act".

(4) In subsection (4), for "section 1 of the Act of 1983" there is substituted "section 7 of the Act of 1992".

10.—(1) Section 337 of that Act is amended as follows.

(2) In subsection (2), for "rights of occupation under the Matrimonial Homes Act 1983" there is substituted "matrimonial home rights under the Family Homes and Domestic Violence Act 1992".

(3) For subsection (3) there is substituted—

"(3) The Act of 1992 has effect, with the necessary modifications, as if—

(a) the rights conferred by paragraph (a) of subsection (2) were matrimonial home rights under that Act,

(b) any application for such leave as is mentioned in that paragraph were an application for an order under section 7 of that Act, and

(c) any charge under paragraph (b) of that subsection on the estate or interest of the trustee were a charge under that Act on the estate or interest of a spouse."

(4) In subsections (4) and (5) for "section 1 of the Act of 1983" there is substituted "section 7 of the Act of 1992".

The Housing Act 1988 (c. 50)

11.—(1) Section 9 of the Housing Act 1988 (extended discretion of court in possession claims) is amended as follows.

(2) In subsection (5)—

(a) in paragraph (a), for "rights of occupation under the Matrimonial Homes Act 1983" there is substituted "matrimonial home rights under the Family Homes and Domestic Violence Act 1992", and

(b) for "those rights of occupation" there is substituted "those matrimonial home rights".

(3) After subsection (5) there is inserted—

"(5A) In any case where—

SCH. 5

(a) at a time when proceedings are brought for possession of a dwelling-house let on an assured tenancy, an order is in force under section 9 of the Family Homes and Domestic Violence Act 1992 conferring rights on a cohabitant or former cohabitant (within the meaning of that Act) or former spouse of the tenant,

(b) that cohabitant, former cohabitant or former spouse is then in occupation of the dwelling-house, and

(c) the assured tenancy is terminated as a result of those proceedings,

the cohabitant, former cohabitant or former spouse shall have the same rights in relation to, or in connection with, any such adjournment as is referred to in subsection (1) above or any such stay, suspension or postponement as is referred to in subsection (2) above as he or she would have if the rights conferred by the order referred to in paragraph (a) above were not affected by the termination of the tenancy."

The Children Act 1989 (c. 41)

12. In section 8(4) of the Children Act 1989 (meaning of "family proceedings" for purposes of that Act) paragraphs (c) and (f) are omitted and at the end there is added—

"(h) the Family Homes and Domestic Violence Act 1992".

The Courts and Legal Services Act 1990 (c. 41)

13. In section 58 of the Courts and Legal Services Act 1990 (conditional fee agreements) in subsection (10) paragraphs (b) and (e) are omitted and immediately before the "or" following paragraph (g) there is inserted—

"(gg) the Family Homes and Domestic Violence Act 1992".

Section 28(2).

SCHEDULE 6

TRANSITIONAL PROVISIONS AND SAVINGS.

Pending applications for orders relating to occupation and molestation

1.—(1) In this paragraph and paragraph 3 "the existing enactments" means—

1976 c. 50.

(a) the Domestic Violence and Matrimonial Proceedings Act 1976,

1978 c. 22.

(b) sections 16 to 18 of the Domestic Proceedings and Magistrates' Courts Act 1978, and

1983 c. 19.

(c) sections 1 and 9 of the Matrimonial Homes Act 1983.

(2) Nothing in this Act shall affect any application for an order or injunction under the existing enactments which is pending immediately before the commencement of this Act.

EXPLANATORY NOTES

Schedule 6

1.   This Schedule deals with the transitional provisions and savings.

Pending applications under Schedule 1 to the Matrimonial Homes Act 1967

2. Nothing in this Act shall affect any application for an order under Schedule 1 to the Matrimonial Homes Act 1983 which is pending immediately before the commencement of this Act.

Existing orders relating to occupation and molestation

3.—(1) In this paragraph "an existing order" means any order or injunction under the existing enactments which—

    (a) is in force immediately before the commmencement of this Act, or

    (b) was made or granted after that commencement in proceedings brought before that commencement.

(2) Subject to sub-paragraphs (3) and (4), nothing in this Act shall—

    (a) prevent an existing order from remaining in force, or

    (b) affect the enforcement of an existing order.

(3) Nothing in this Act shall affect any application to extend, vary or discharge an existing order, but the court may, if it thinks it just and reasonable to do so, treat the application as an application for an order under this Act.

(4) The making of an order under this Act between parties with respect to whom an existing order is in force discharges the existing order.

Matrimonial home rights

4. Any reference in any enactment, instrument or document (whether passed or made before or after the passing of this Act) to rights of occupation within the meaning of the Matrimonial Homes Act 1983 shall, in relation to any time after the commencement of this Act, be construed as being or as the case requires including a reference to matrimonial home rights within the meaning of this Act.

Cautions lodged before 14th February 1983

5. References in this Act to registration under section 5(6) include (as well as references to registration by notice under section 2(7) of the Matrimonial Homes Act 1967 or section 2(8) of the Matrimonial Homes Act 1983) references to registration by caution duly lodged under section 2(7) of the Matrimonial Homes Act 1967 before 14th February 1983 (the date of the commencement of section 4(2) of the Matrimonial Homes and Property Act 1981).

6. Neither section 5(7) of this Act nor the repeal by the Matrimonial Homes and Property Act 1981 of the words "or caution" in section 2(7) of the Matrimonial Homes Act 1967, affects any caution duly lodged as respects any estate or interest before 14th February 1981.

SCHEDULE 7

REPEALS

Chapter	Short title	Extent of repeal
1976 c. 50.	The Domestic Violence and Matrimonial Proceedings Act 1976.	The whole Act.
1978 c. 22.	The Domestic Proceedings and Magistrates' Courts Act 1978.	Sections 16 to 18. Section 28(2). In Schedule 2, paragraph 53.
1983 c. 19.	The Matrimonial Homes Act 1983.	The whole Act.
1985 c. 61.	The Administration of Justice Act 1985.	In section 34(2), paragraph (f) and the word "and" immediately preceding it.
1985 c. 71.	The Housing (Consequential Provisions) Act 1985.	In Schedule 2, paragraph 56.
1988 c. 50.	The Housing Act 1988.	In Schedule 17, paragraphs 33 and 34.
1989 c. 41.	The Children Act 1989.	Section 8(4)(c) and (f).
1990 c. 41.	The Courts and Legal Services Act 1990.	Section 58(10)(b) and (e). In Schedule 18, paragraph 21.

EXPLANATORY NOTES

Schedule 7

1.   This Schedule deals with repeals.

2.   The major repeals are of the Domestic Violence and Matrimonial Proceedings Act 1976, the Matrimonial Homes Act 1983 and sections 16 to 18 of the Domestic Proceedings and Magistrates' Courts Act 1978.

APPENDIX B

LIST OF NATIONAL ORGANISATIONS WHO RESPONDED TO WORKING PAPER NO. 113

Association of Chief Police Officers
Association of County Councils
Association of Women Solicitors
Children's Legal Centre
Children's Society
Church Commissioners
Council of H.M. Circuit Judges
Department of Health
Family Law Bar Association
Family Rights Group
Institute of Legal Executives
Justices' Clerks' Society
Law Society
Magistrates' Association
Metropolitan Police
National Children's Bureau
National Council for One Parent Families
National Family Trust
National Farmers' Union
National Society for the Prevention of Cruelty to Children
Network
Police Superintendents' Association
Rights of Women
Society of Conservative Lawyers
Society of County Secretaries
Solicitors' Family Law Association
Welsh Women's Aid
Women's Aid Federation (England)
Women's National Commission

LIST OF LOCAL ORGANISATIONS WHO RESPONDED TO WORKING PAPER NO. 113

Chester Ratepayers Party
Director of Housing, Sheffield City Council
London Housing Unit
London Women's Aid

LIST OF INDIVIDUALS WHO RESPONDED TO WORKING PAPER NO. 113

N.F. Allen
Chris Barton
Professor Stephen Cretney
Gillian Douglas
Dr Susan Edwards
His Honour Judge Fricker Q.C.
David Gough
Her Honour Jean Graham Hall
Ann Halpern
Mary Hayes J.P.
Mr Registrar Greenslade
Hodge, Jones and Allen
C.T. Latham, stipendiary magistrate
Bruce Lidington
Douglas Martin
Professor Jill Martin
B. Mizen
Occupiers of 18 Chapman Street
Martin Parry
Margaret Peasegood and Co.
His Honour Judge Stannard
Mrs Naomi Turner
J. Whybrow

Printed in the United Kingdom for HMSO
Dd 5067015 10/95 C1 51-0-0 50423 ON 335093